Highlighting the Good News
(A Witness Companion To The Holy Bible)

Selected,

(KJV)

Abbreviated, Paraphrased, and Edited

Focused Like A Laser's Beam

For

Youth,
Adults, Pastors,
Leaders, Families, Military,
Worship, Evangelism, Missions,
Scripture Memory, Inspiration, Devotions,
Schools, Libraries, Hospitals, Prisons, Office,
Pew, Desktop, Weddings,
Awards, Gifts,

You

by
Brian L. Birch

𝓗𝓲𝓰𝓱𝓵𝓲𝓰𝓱𝓽𝓲𝓷𝓰 𝓽𝓱𝓮 𝓖𝓸𝓸𝓭 𝓝𝓮𝔀𝓼
Copyrighted 2009
by Brian L. Birch
St. Paul, Minnesota 55118-4335, USA
thegoodnews@q.com

Holy Bible, King James Version (KJV)
Selected, Abbreviated, Paraphrased, and Edited
by Brian L. Birch

Library of Congress Number: 2009940461

ISBN Number: 978-0-9754031-1-2

Cover Illustration by
Carole Kinion-Copeland © 2008
Oronoco, Minnesota, 55960, USA
Natural Science Illustrator
Member of Guild of Natural Science Illustrators

Butterfly symbolizes change, resurrection and a new life
White Rose symbolizes love and beauty
Cover illustration was chosen for its artistry

FOREWORD

I wrote this book because there is a need for understanding Christianity. I have studied the *Bible* since my youth. In 1984 I founded a ministry in Jamaica named Project Increase, which still continues after twenty-six years.

I have been overseas 47 times leading groups on evangelism and work projects. I have been in homes that serve the needs of boys and girls, in youth and adult prisons, and worked improving churches, schools, etc.. I have personally given *Bibles* to many people. Unfortunately, I discovered that because of the time it takes to read the whole *Bible*, many people did not read it all, or even large sections of it.

God's Word is such an inspiration to me that I want to make the heart of its message available for any person to read in a short time. There is much value in doing so. I wish I had a book like this *Highlighting the Good News* available when I was very young. Even now in my senior years, I am excited by this condensed message that is so refreshing and filled with hope and assurance. This book is truly a timeless book for all ages.

The brief transition statements I made introducing the different books within *Highlighting the Good News* are for aiding those who have never read the *Bible* or are not very familiar with it. There are many verses in the Old Testament where the words *I, he,* and *my* are used. In most cases these refer to God or the Lord Jesus Christ speaking. This will become evident as you read. In the New Testament *I, he,* or *my* usually refer to Jesus Christ, the Holy Spirit, or God, interchangeably. In a few cases I have chosen to clarify who is speaking.

My goal in writing *Highlighting the Good News* was to condense the central message of the *Bible* in such a way that readers could easily comprehend it in several days, not months or years. I believe that *Highlighting the Good News* offers readers the opportunity to read and feel the impact of God's Word on their lives almost immediately. It is capable of speaking for itself.

Highlighting the Good News follows the *Bible*'s time line of events so that a person can understand God's personal dealings with mankind. I began *Highlighting the Good News* with Genesis and kept all the books in order. This first book is historical background in abbreviated form so that readers will benefit by getting to know about creation, man's beginnings, and early history. The *Bible* tells us the truth about creation and all biblical events thereafter.

Highlighting the Good News serves as a stepping stone leading to faith and discussion. This book puts the entire *Holy Bible* into perspective and encourages further interest in it. Because of the condensed content, *Highlighting the Good News* is very helpful for topic or word studies, as well as for sharing the Christian faith. All other religions of the world should test the *Bible* for truth by comparing it honestly side by side with their guiding documents. The *Bible* will prove to be far superior to all other comparisons because it has no equal; it is holy and it rejects contrary doctrine.

Highlighting the Good News' selected scriptures can become teaching aids for families. I encourage you to use these passages to train up children in the way they should live their lives, and they will not likely depart from them.

My prayer is that *Highlighting the Good News* will minister to you as you read it. I encourage you to write in the margins by the passages that are significant to you. I am confident that you will find this book a useful tool when sharing God's Word with others.

There is a new hymn by Lynn DeShazo, *Ancient Words,* that I highly recommend you listen to. It is a magnificent Call to Worship and worth memorizing. The words express many of my feelings as I wrote this book.

May God bless you richly as you study His Word.

Brian L. Birch, Author

TABLE OF CONTENTS

OLD TESTAMENT

NEW TESTAMENT

Highlighting the Good News

(A Witness Companion To The Holy Bible)

(KJV)
Selected, Abbreviated, Paraphrased, and Edited

OLD TESTAMENT

Genesis

Zero plus zero always equals zero, so in a way, that helps explain why God's *Bible* is so needful. It contains man's best answer to life and our beginning. No person can comprehend God's eternal existence. God must have always existed from eternity past for anything to exist in the first place.

God says he has no needs, so if God has no needs and can create anything, he certainly can give us his Word to read in answer to our desire to know our beginnings. God has also said he has put the concept of time in our minds.

No big bang or evolution theory comes remotely close to giving us logical explanations of our beginnings. But the book of Genesis is about the beginnings of our universe and our life as we know it. It is about man's coming into existence and our relationship to the God who created us. Logically, God cannot have a beginning, or be more than one. It is we who do not understand.

Genesis 1   Creation

1 In the beginning God created the heavens and the earth.
3 And God said, Let there be light, and there was light, making the first day.
6 Then God said, Let there be sky, and let it divide the heaven's waters from the earth's waters, making the second day.
11 Next God said, Let the earth bring forth vegetation, the herb yielding seed and the fruit tree yielding fruit after its kind, making the third day.
14 Then God said, Let there be lights in the sky to divide the day from the night, and let them be for seasons, days, and years, making the fourth day.
20 And God said, Let the waters bring forth sea creatures abundantly and birds that fly in the earth's sky, making the fifth day.

22 The LORD God said, Behold, the man has become as one of <u>us</u>, to know good and evil. Now, if he eats of the tree of life, he will live forever.

23 Therefore, the LORD God sent them out of the Garden of Eden.

24 Then God said, Let the earth bring forth living creatures and animals after its kind.

26-27 Last, God said, Let us make man in our image, after our likeness, and let them have dominion over the fish of the sea, the birds of the air, over the animals of the earth, and over every creeping thing on the earth. So God created man in his own likeness, male and female.

31 Then God saw everything that he had made, and behold, it was very good, making the sixth day.

Notice in verse 26-27, God said, "Let <u>us</u> make man in <u>our</u> image." That is the first reference in the *Bible* about the nature of our triune God.

Genesis 2

2 On the seventh day, God, having ended this creation, rested.

3 God blessed the seventh day and designated it as sanctified (holy).

7 The LORD God formed man out of the dust of the ground, he breathed into him the breath of life, and man became a living soul.

8 God planted a garden eastward in Eden, and there he put man.

9 And out of the ground grew every tree that is pleasant and good for food, plus the tree of life and the tree of knowledge of good and evil.

16-17 God commanded man, saying, Of every tree of the garden you may freely eat, but of the tree of knowledge of good and evil, you shall not eat of it, for in the day that you eat from it, you shall surely die.

22 Then, God took from man one of his ribs and made a woman.

Genesis 3

1, 3,4 Later, in the Garden of Eden, there was a particular serpent that said to the woman, Has God said, you shall not eat of every tree of the garden? The woman answered, God has commanded me, You shall not eat of the tree of knowledge, neither shall you touch it, or you shall die. So the serpent enticed the woman, saying, You shall not surely die.

6-9 The woman disobeyed God, believed the serpent, took of the forbidden fruit and ate it, and then she gave some to her husband, Adam, and he ate, also. The eyes of them both were opened, and they knew that they were naked. And when they heard the voice of the LORD God, they hid themselves from his presence. The LORD God called Adam and said, Where are you?

10-12 Adam said, I heard your voice and was afraid because I was naked, so I hid myself. And God said, Who told you that you were naked? Have you

eaten of the tree of knowledge? Then Adam said, The woman whom you gave me, she gave me of the tree, and I did eat.
20 Adam named his wife Eve because she would be the mother of all people.

Genesis 6

1-3 Some time later, when mankind began to multiply on earth and daughters were born to them, the sons who respected God saw that the daughters of mankind were fair, and they took them as wives as they chose. The LORD said, My spirit shall not always strive with man, for he is also mortal flesh.
5 God saw that the wickedness of man was great on the earth, and that every imagination of the thoughts of his heart were always evil.
8 But the man Noah found grace in the eyes of the LORD.
9 Noah was a just man and perfect in his generations; he walked with God.
11 The earth was corrupt in God's sight, and it was filled with violence.
12-13 God looked upon the earth, and it was corrupt, for all mankind had corrupted God's ways. God said to Noah, I will destroy them with the earth.
14 Noah made an ark of gopher wood. (This was about 1656 years after the creation of the earth and Adam and Eve.)
17-19 God said, Behold, I will bring a flood of waters upon the earth to destroy all flesh, and everything that is on the earth shall die. But I will establish my covenant with Noah, and he shall come into the ark with his family, and two of every living creature of all flesh, one male and one female.

Genesis 7

4 God said, I will cause it to rain 40 days and 40 nights, and every living creature shall be destroyed.
24 And the waters remained upon the earth 150 days after the flood.

Genesis 8

21-22 After the rain, the LORD said in his heart, I will not curse the ground anymore, for the imagination of man's heart is evil from his youth; I will not strike every living creature as I have done. While the earth remains, seedtime and harvest, summer and winter, day and night shall not cease.

Genesis 9

5-6 God said, Whoever sheds man's blood, by man shall his blood be shed, for man was made in the image of God.
16-17 The rainbow shall be in the sky, and I will look upon it so that I

may remember this everlasting covenant between myself and every living creature of all flesh that is upon the earth.

Genesis 12

1-3 (Now begins the story of Abram. He was born about 1,948 years after creation and 291 years after Noah) The LORD said to Abram, Get out of your country and from your kindred and father's house. Go into a land that I will show you, and I will make of you a great nation. I will bless you and make your name great. You shall be a blessing, and I will bless those who bless you and curse those who curse you, and in you shall all the families of earth be blessed.

Genesis 15

6 Abram believed in God, and he counted Abram's faith as righteousness.

Genesis 17

1-2 When Abram was 99 years old, the LORD appeared to him and said, I am the Almighty God. Walk before me, and be perfect. I will make my covenant between you and me, and I will multiply you exceedingly.
7-8 I will establish my covenant as an everlasting covenant, and I will be your God. I will give to you and your children all the land of Canaan for an everlasting possession, and I will be your God. (God renamed Abram shortly thereafter and called him Abraham.)

Exodus

Later, Moses became the new leader of the Israelite people and led them out of Egyptian bondage. The book of Exodus is the story of Moses plus two events: the Passover and the parting of the Red Sea. (The Exodus event happened around 2515 years after Creation. This now dovetails into secular history that dates back to about 1220 years BC. Ramasses II was the most famous Pharaoh around this time period. So, the addition of the two above dates plus our present year AD gives us the approximate years from Creation to this year. Other historical events that come later in the whole Bible reconfirm this conclusion. (I say this for the purpose of refuting the "Evolution" and "Big Bang" theories that are being pushed upon us today.)

Exodus 3

13-14 Moses said to God, When I stand before the children of Israel (the nation) and say to them, The God of your forefathers has sent me to you. They shall reply, What is his name? What shall I then say to them? So God said to Moses, say, I AM who I AM. Tell them, I AM has sent me to you.
15 And God said to Moses, Say to the children of Israel, the LORD God of your forefathers, the God of Abraham, Isaac, and Jacob has sent me to you.

Exodus 6

2 And God spoke to Moses, and said to him, I am Yahweh (Jehovah), the LORD.

Exodus 12   The Passover event

13 God said, Blood shall be to you a sign upon your houses. When I see the blood, I will pass over you. The plague shall not come upon you to destroy you when I inflict death upon the land of Egypt.
14 This day shall become a memorial to you, and you shall keep it as a feast to the LORD throughout your generations and forever.
29 So it came to pass, that at midnight the LORD struck dead all the first-born in the land of Egypt: of Pharaoh, of the captive, and of the cattle.
42 The Passover event is a night to be observed as a reminder of the LORD bringing the Israelites out of bondage from the land of Egypt.

Exodus 15

1-2 Then sang Moses and the children of Israel this song to the LORD: I will sing to the LORD, for he has triumphed gloriously; the horse and his rider he has thrown into the sea. The LORD is my strength and my song. He has become my salvation and my God. I will prepare him a habitation, and I will exalt him.
3 The LORD is a man of war; Yahweh is his name.
6-7 Your right hand, oh LORD, has become glorious in power and has dashed the enemy into pieces. In the greatness of your excellency you have overthrown those who rose up against you. You sent your wrath and it consumed them.
11 Who is like you, oh LORD, among the gods? Who is like you, glorious in holiness, fearful in praises, and doing wonders?
13 In your mercy you have led the people whom you have redeemed. You have guided them in your strength to your holy habitation.
18 The LORD shall reign forever and ever.

Exodus 18

11 Now I know that the LORD is greater than all gods, for as the Egyptians were proud of their gods, the LORD was above them all.

Exodus 20   The Ten Commandments.

3 You shall have no other gods before me.
4 You shall not make any man-made image that has any likeness of any thing that is in heaven above, or on earth below, or in the waters of the earth.
7 You shall not take the name of the LORD your God in vain, for the LORD will not hold anyone guiltless who does so.
8 Remember the sabbath day, to keep it holy.
12 Honor your father and mother that your days may be long upon the earth which the LORD your God gives you.
13 You shall not kill.
14 You shall not commit adultery.
15 You shall not steal.
16 You shall not bear false witness against your neighbor.
17 You shall not covet your neighbor's house, nor your neighbor's wife, nor anything that is your neighbor's.

Exodus 23

1 You shall not give a false report to aid wicked people.
2 You shall not follow the crowd to do evil; do not speak to bend the truth.
3 Neither shall you favor unjustly a poor man in his cause.
6 You shall not deny justice to the poor.
7 Keep yourself far from a false matter; do not harm the innocent and righteous person.
8 You shall take no gift, for it blinds the wise and perverts the words of the righteous.
9 You shall not oppress foreigners; relate to them wisely.
10 Six years you shall plant your land and gather its fruits. But the seventh year you shall let your land rest so that your people may eat, and what remains, leave for the animals to eat.
12 Six days you shall do your work. On the seventh day you shall rest, along with all others, that all the people may be refreshed.
13 In all things that I have said to you, be wise and make no mention of the names of other gods.
19 You shall bring the results of the first fruits of your labors into the house of the LORD your God.

25 You shall serve the LORD your God, and he will bless your bread and your water. He will take sickness away from the people.

Exodus 31

13 Moses, speak to the children of Israel, saying, Keep my sabbaths, for it is a sign between you and me throughout your generations that you may know that I am the LORD who sanctifies you (makes you holy).

Exodus 34

14 You shall worship no other gods, for the LORD, whose name is Jealous, is a jealous God.
15 Beware not to make a covenant with others and go lusting after their gods.
17 You shall not make for yourself any self-molded gods.
20 Nobody shall appear before me empty of an offering to me.
21 Six days you shall work, but on the seventh day you shall rest.
26 The best of the first fruits of your labor you shall bring into the house of the LORD your God.

Exodus 35

2 Six days shall work be done, but on the seventh day there shall be a holy day, a sabbath day of rest to the LORD.

Leviticus

God uses the book of Leviticus to instruct those who choose to yield to God's love and commands. The Ten Commandments are re-emphasized.

Leviticus 11

45 I am the LORD, I am to be your God; you shall be holy, for I am holy.

Leviticus 19

11 You shall not steal; neither deceive nor lie one to another.
12 You shall not swear by my name falsely; neither shall you profane the name of your God, for I am the LORD.
13 You shall not defraud your neighbor, nor rob him. Do not delay his wages.

14 You shall not curse the deaf, nor cause the blind to stumble, but fear your God, for I am the LORD.

15 You shall not be unrighteousness in judgment.

16 You shall not go about gossiping among your people; I am the LORD.

17 You shall not hate people in your heart. You shall not rebuke your neighbor nor cause him harm.

18 You shall not take revenge nor bear a grudge, but you shall love your neighbor as yourself; I am the LORD.

37 You shall observe all my statutes and my judgments; I am the LORD.

Leviticus 26

12 I will walk among you and be your God, and you shall be my people.

Numbers

Numbers is about our relationship with God and how he cares for us.

Numbers 6

24 The LORD bless you and keep you.

25 The LORD make his face shine upon you and be gracious to you.

26 The LORD lift up his countenance upon you and give you his peace.

Numbers 10

35 Rise up, LORD, and let your enemies be scattered.

Numbers 14

18 The LORD is long suffering and of great mercy, forgiving iniquity and transgressions, but by no means clearing the guilty, putting iniquity of the fathers upon his children to the third and fourth generations.

Numbers 23

19 God is not a man, that he should lie; neither the son of man, that he should repent. What he has said, he will do, and he will make it good.

23 Who can live if it is outside of God's will?

Deuteronomy

In the book of Deuteronomy, God draws a line; he demonstrates his standards to be so high that we must conclude that he is absolutely holy, and we are not. Inwardly we are choosing whom we will follow, God or ourselves.

The Ten Commandments, again, reflect God's holiness and show us the need for a savior and the importance of following the Word of the Lord.

Deuteronomy 4

23 Beware that you do not forget the covenant of the LORD and make false idols, which the LORD your God has forbidden.
24 The LORD your God is a consuming fire and a jealous God.
29 If you seek the LORD your God with all your heart and with all your soul, you shall find him.
30 When you are troubled, and all these things have come upon you, turn to the LORD your God, and be obedient to his voice.
31 The LORD is a merciful God; he will not forsake you nor destroy you; do not forget the covenant he made with your fathers.
35 To you it was shown, that you might know the LORD is God; there is no other beside him.
39 Know this day in your heart that the LORD is God. In heaven above and upon the earth below; there is no other.
40 You shall keep God's statutes and commandments, which I command you, that it may be well with you and with your children, so that you may live long upon the earth, which the LORD your God gives you forever.

Deuteronomy 5

6 I am the LORD your God, who brought you out of bondage.
7 You shall have no other gods before me.
8 You shall not make for yourself any hand-made image that has a likeness in heaven above, or on the earth below, or in the waters of the earth.
9 You shall not bow down to them nor serve them, for I the LORD your God am a jealous God, putting iniquity of the fathers upon his children to the third and fourth generations of those who hate me.

10 I will show mercy to thousands of those who love me and keep my commandments.

11 You shall not take the name of the LORD your God in vain, for the LORD will not hold those guiltless who take his name in vain.

12 Keep the sabbath day holy as the LORD your God has commanded.

16 Honor your father and your mother as the LORD your God has commanded, that your days may be long, and it may go well with you.

17 You shall not kill.

18 Neither shall you commit adultery.

19 Neither shall you steal.

20 Neither shall you bear false witness against your neighbor.

21 Neither shall you desire your neighbor's wife, nor your neighbor's house or his possessions.

Deuteronomy 6

4 Listen, the LORD our God is one LORD!

5 You shall love the LORD your God with all your heart, soul, and might.

6-7, 9 These words which I command you this day shall be in your heart. Teach them diligently to your children, and talk of them when you sit in your home and when you walk outdoors all day long. You shall write them upon your house as a public testimony.

13 You shall fear the LORD your God and serve him. You shall affirm truth by his name.

14-15 You shall not go after other gods, for the LORD your God is a jealous God. If you go after other gods, the anger of the LORD will come against you and destroy you from the face of the earth.

16 You shall not tempt the LORD your God.

17 You shall diligently keep the commandments of the LORD your God. You shall keep his testimonies and his statutes, which he commands you.

Deuteronomy 7

26 Neither shall you bring an abomination into your house, or you will be cursed like it, but you shall greatly detest it, for it is a cursed thing.

Deuteronomy 8

18 Remember the LORD your God, for it is he who gives you power to get wealth.

19 If you forget the LORD your God and walk after other gods to serve and worship them, I testify against you this day that you shall surely perish.

Deuteronomy 9

17-18 I took the Ten Commandments, cast them out of my hands, and broke them before your eyes. I fell down before the LORD. I did not eat bread or drink water because of all your sins of wickedness in the sight of the LORD. They provoked him to anger.

21 I took your sin, the idol which you had made like a calf, and burned it in the fire; next I smashed it to the ground and into dust; then I cast the dust into the creek to be carried away.

Deuteronomy 12

3-4 Cut down the carved images of their gods and destroy their names from that place. You shall not worship the LORD with such things.

28 Observe and hear all these words which I command you, that it may go well with you and with your children forever when you do that which is good and right in the sight of the LORD your God.

30 Take notice that you are not snared by following after their gods.

31 You shall not do so to the LORD, for he hates the abominations they have done with their gods.

32 Observe to do as I command you; do not add nor subtract from them.

Deuteronomy 15

6 The LORD blesses you as he promised. You shall lend to many nations but not borrow. You shall reign over many nations, but they shall not reign over you.

Deuteronomy 22

5 A woman shall not wear a man's clothing; neither shall a man put on woman's clothing, for all who do are an abomination to the LORD your God.

Deuteronomy 32

3 Because I proclaim the name of the LORD, people attribute greatness to our God.

4 God is the Rock. His work is perfect; he is a God of truth and purity.

Deuteronomy 33

26 There is none like God. He rides upon the heavens to help you.

11

27 The eternal God is your refuge, and underneath are his everlasting arms. He shall throw out your enemy.

Joshua

Joshua confirms God's incomparable holiness.

Joshua 1

8 The book of the law shall not depart from your mouth; you shall meditate on it day and night. Do according to all that is written in it, and then you shall become prosperous and have good success.
9 Be strong and of good courage; be not afraid. Neither be dismayed, for the LORD your God is with you wherever you go.

Joshua 5

15 The captain of the LORD's army said to Joshua, Take off your shoes, for the place where you are standing is holy ground.

Joshua 22

5 Follow the commandments and the laws. Love the LORD God and walk in all his ways. Hold fast to him and serve him with all your heart and soul.
22 The LORD is the God of gods.

Joshua 24

18-19 The LORD drove out the enemy. We will serve the LORD, for he is our God. He is a jealous God.
20 If you forsake the LORD and serve strange gods, he will do you harm and consume you, even though he has been good to you.
24 We will serve the LORD our God; we will obey his voice.

Judges

Serving any god that is not God cannot benefit you, despite what you may think.

Judges 10

13 The LORD said, You have forsaken me and served other gods; wherefore I will deliver you no more.

14 Go and cry to the gods which you have chosen; let them deliver you in the time of your tribulation.

Ruth

What Ruth is speaking to Naomi is worthy of being our attitude toward God.

Ruth 1

16 Wherever you go, I will go, and wherever you lodge, I will lodge. Your people shall be my people, and your God, my God.

1 Samuel

In 1st Samuel, God establishes, again, that he is holy and sovereign.

1 Samuel 2

2 There is none holy as the LORD, for there is none his equal; neither is there any rock like our God.

3 Do not be exceedingly proud; let no arrogance come out of your mouth, for the LORD is a God of knowledge, and by him your actions are weighed.

6 The LORD kills and gives life; he brings you down into the grave, and he brings you up out of it.

7 The LORD makes you poor or rich; he brings you low or lifts you up.

8 The pillars of the earth are the LORD's, and he has set the world upon them.

10 The enemies of the LORD shall be broken to pieces; out of heaven shall thunder come upon them. The LORD shall judge all the earth, and he shall exalt his anointed.

2 Samuel

God's foundation is truth. God is personal and a shield for his people.

2 Samuel 22

2 The LORD is my rock, my fortress, and my deliverer.
3 In him will I trust. He is my Shield, my Salvation, my High Tower, my Refuge, and my Savior.
4 I will call on the LORD, who is worthy to be praised; so shall I be saved from my enemies.
7 In my distress I called upon the LORD. He heard my voice out of his temple, and my cry entered his ears.
21 The LORD rewarded me according to my righteousness; according to the cleanliness of my hands has he rewarded me.
22 I have kept the ways of the LORD and not departed from my God.
25 Therefore, the LORD has rewarded me according to my righteousness, according to my cleanliness in his eye sight.
29 You are my lamp, oh LORD, and you light up my darkness.
30 By you I have run through my enemy's army; by my God I have leaped over a wall.
31 As for God, his ways are perfect; the Word of the LORD is tried. He is a shield to all who trust in him.
32 Who is God, except the LORD, and who is a rock, except our God?
33 God is my strength and power. He makes my way perfect.
47 The LORD lives. Exalted be the God of the rock of my salvation.
48-49 It is God who avenges me. He brings me away from my enemies; he has lifted me high above them; he has delivered me from the violent man.

2 Samuel 24

14 I am in trouble; let us now fall into the hands of the LORD, for his mercies are great; let us not fall into the hands of man.

1 Kings

There is no God like this God, as described in the *Bible*.

1 Kings 8

23 LORD God of Israel, there is no God like you in heaven above or on earth below. You keep your covenant and have mercy on your servants who walk before you with their whole heart.
27 Will God dwell on the earth? Behold, the heaven and heaven of heavens cannot contain you, much less this house that I have built.

14

58 Give your heart to God; walk in all his ways, and keep his commandments, his statutes, and his judgments, which he commands.

1 Kings 18

39 The LORD, he is God.

2 Kings (not used)

1 Chronicles

1st and 2nd Chronicles tell us we can rejoice in God, who alone is God.

1 Chronicles 16

8 Give thanks to the LORD; call upon his name; make known his deeds among the people.
9 Sing to him; sing psalms to him; talk of all his wondrous works.
10 Glory in his holy name; let the heart of those who rejoice seek the LORD.
11 Seek the LORD and his strength. Seek his face continually.
12 Remember the marvellous works that God has done, remember his wonders and the judgments of his mouth.
23 Sing to the LORD, all the earth; show forth from day to day his salvation.
24 Declare his glory and his marvelous works among all nations.
25 Great is the LORD and greatly to be praised; he also is to be feared above all gods.
28 Give to the LORD, you people; give to the LORD glory and strength.
29 Give to the LORD the glory due his name; bring an offering and come before him; worship the LORD in the beauty of holiness.
31 Let the heavens be glad, and let the earth rejoice. Let men say among the nations, the LORD reigns.
34 Give thanks to the LORD, for he is good. His mercy endures forever.
35 Say, Save us, oh God of our salvation, and gather us together. Deliver us from the heathen, that we may give thanks to your holy name and glory in your praise.
36 Blessed be the LORD God of Israel forever and ever, and all the people said, Amen, and praised the LORD.

1 Chronicles 17

20 LORD, there is none like you; neither is there any God other than you.

15

2 Chronicles 5

13 It came to be, as the trumpeters and singers were praising and thanking the LORD, they lifted up their voice with the trumpets, cymbals and instruments of music and praised the LORD, saying, For he is good. His mercy endures forever. The house of the LORD was filled with a cloud.

2 Chronicles 15

2 The LORD is with you when you are with him. If you seek him, you will find him, but if you reject him, he will reject you.

2 Chronicles 18

13 As the LORD lives, even what my God says, that will I speak.

2 Chronicles 19

7 Let the fear of the LORD be upon you, for there is no iniquity with the LORD our God. He does not unjustly favor persons or take bribes.

2 Chronicles 20

6 LORD God of our fathers, are you not our God in heaven? Nobody is able to overcome you.
21 Praise the LORD, for his mercy endures forever.

2 Chronicles 30

18-19 The good LORD pardons everyone who prepares their heart to seek God.

Ezra

God's Word is encouraging, as well as instructive, about God's view of sin.

Ezra 8

22 The hand of our God is upon all who seek him for good, but his power and wrath are against all who forsake him.

Ezra 9

13 After all that has come upon us for our evil ways, our God has punished us less than we deserve, and he has delivered us.

Ezra 10

11 Make confession to the LORD God of your fathers, and do his pleasure. Separate yourselves from wayward people and pagan wives where you live.

Nehemiah

This is more good news from God's Word.

Nehemiah 1

5-6 The LORD God of heaven, the great and awesome God, he keeps his covenants and has mercy on those who love him and observe his commandments, hear the prayers of your servant, which I pray day and night.

Nehemiah 9

5-6 Stand up and bless the LORD your God forever and ever. Blessed be your glorious name; you are exalted above all blessings and praise. You are the LORD alone; you have made heaven, the heaven of heavens, the earth, and all things that are in them. You preserve them all, and those in heaven worship you.

Esther (not used)

Job

God is almighty. Man is accountable for not giving proper respect to God and for not yielding to God's Word.

Job 8

3-5 Does Almighty God distort judgment? Seek God early, and make your plea to the Almighty.
9 We are but a segment of history and really know nothing.
15 We may lean upon our house, but it shall not stand; we shall hold it fast, but it shall not endure.
20 God will not cast away a perfect man. He will not help those who do evil.
22 Those who hate God shall be clothed with shame, and the dwelling place of the wicked shall come to nothing.

Job 9

32 God is not a man, as I am, that I can debate his judgment.

Job 12

13 With God is wisdom and strength; he has counsel and understanding.

Job 19

25 I know that my Redeemer lives, and that he shall stand at the last day upon the earth. Worms will destroy my body, yet in my flesh shall I see God, whom I shall see for myself and behold, and not another.

Job 22

21 Acquaint yourself with God, and be at peace; thereby good shall come to you. Receive the law from his mouth, and lay up his words in your heart.

Job 25

2 Dominion and fear are with God. He makes peace where he is.
4 How can man be justified with God, or how can man be sinless who is born of a woman?
5 Behold, even the moon and the stars are not pure in his sight.

Job 28

28 To man God said, Behold, the fear of the LORD is wisdom, and to depart from evil is understanding.

Job 33

4 The spirit of God has made me, and the breath of the Almighty has given me life.

Job 36

5 God is mighty and despises no one. He is mighty in strength and wisdom.

Job 37

23 By touching the Almighty, we cannot know him altogether. He is excellent in power and in judgment.

Psalms

The book of Psalms is a book of songs. They magnify the Lord God, and by reading them, we find that man is incapable of being equal to God. All we can do is reflect God's influence in our lives. Psalms is located in the very middle of the *Bible*. How unique is God's Word. Chapter 118 is the middle chapter of the *Bible*. The shortest chapter in the *Bible* is in front of it, chapter 117. The longest chapter in the *Bible*, chapter 119, is right after it. If you add up all the chapters before and after chapter 118, your total is 1188! Surprisingly, it is Psalm 118:8 that is the exact middle verse of the *Bible,* too. Psalm 118:8 reads, "It is better to take refuge in the Lord than to trust in people." How true that is!

Now read the inspirational songs by those who knew God's love and endeavored to follow these songs' teachings. Here is much wisdom. Psalms is about who God is and what our personal relationship with God can be. God offers us his best. We can choose to honor God, or we can turn our backs on his love to follow the world's ways by living selfishly for ourselves.

Psalm 2

11 Serve the LORD with respectful fear, and rejoice with trembling.

Psalm 3

3 You, oh LORD, are a shield for me. You are my glory and the one who lifts up my head.

Psalm 4

4 Stand in awe, and sin not; commune with your own heart upon your bed, and be still.
8 I will rest in peace and sleep, for only the LORD makes me safe.

Psalm 5

3 My voice shall you hear in the morning, oh LORD; I will direct my prayer to you and look up.
4 You are not a God who takes pleasure in wickedness; neither shall evil dwell with you.
5 The foolish shall not stand in your sight; you hate all workers of iniquity.
12 You, oh LORD, will bless the righteous; with favor you will surround us like a shield.

Psalm 6

9 The LORD has heard my plea; the LORD will receive my prayer.

Psalm 7

9 Let wickedness come to an end. Establish the just, for God's righteousness tests the heart of man.
11 God judges the righteous person and is angry with the wicked everyday.
12 If man turns not, God will sharpen his sword, bend his bow and take aim.
17 I will praise the LORD according to his righteousness, and I will sing praise to the name of the LORD most high.

Psalm 8

1 Oh LORD, our Lord, how excellent is thy name in all the earth! You have set your glory above the heavens.
3-5 When I consider your heavens, the work of your fingers, the moon and the stars, which you have ordained, what is man, that you art mindful of him, and the son of man, that you visit him? You have made him a little lower than the angels, and have crowned him with glory and honor.

Psalm 9

7 The LORD shall endure forever; he has prepared his throne for judgment.
9 The LORD will be a refuge for the oppressed, a refuge in times of trouble.

Psalm 12

6 The words of the LORD are pure words, as silver is purified in a furnace, but seven times more.

Psalm 13

5 I have trusted in God's mercy; my heart shall rejoice in his salvation.
6 I will sing to the LORD because he has acted bountifully with me.

Psalm 14

2 The LORD looked down from heaven upon the children of men to see if there were any who did understand and seek God.
3 They all had gone astray; they were altogether corrupt. Not one does good.

Psalm 16

4 Men's sorrow shall be multiplied who quickly go after another god.
5 The LORD is the portion of my inheritance and of my cup; he maintains my life.
8 I always set the LORD before me. Because he is at my right hand, I shall not be moved.

Psalm 17

6 I have called upon God. He says, Incline your ear to me and hear my voice.
7 Show your marvelous loving kindness, oh God. You save by your right hand those who put their trust in you.

Psalm 18

2 The LORD is my rock, my fortress and my deliverer. He is my strength in whom I will trust, my shield, and the sound of my salvation. He is my high tower of safety.
30 As for God, his way is perfect; the Word of the LORD is tested; he is a shield to all who trust in him.
31 Who is God except the LORD, or who is a rock except our God?
32 It is God who girds me with strength and makes my way perfect.
46 The LORD lives. Blessed be my rock. Let the God of my salvation be exalted.

Psalm 19

1 The heavens declare the glory of God, and the skies show his creativity.
7 The law of the LORD is perfect, converting the soul; the testimony of the LORD is sure, making wise the simple.
8 The statutes of the LORD are right, rejoicing the heart; the commandments of the LORD are pure, enlightening the eyes.
9 The fear of the LORD is clean, enduring forever; the judgments of the LORD are true and righteous altogether.
14 Let the words of my mouth and the meditation of my heart be acceptable in your sight, oh LORD, my strength and my redeemer.

Psalm 22

23 You who fear the LORD, praise him, glorify him, and fear him, all you descendants of Israel.

Psalm 23

1, 3, 6 The LORD is my shepherd; I shall be satisfied. He restores my soul; he leads me in the paths of righteousness for his name's sake. Surely goodness and mercy shall follow me all the days of my life, and I will dwell in the house of the LORD forever.

Psalm 24

1 The earth is the LORD's and the fullness of it, the world and those who dwell on it.
8 Who is this King of glory? The LORD strong and mighty, the LORD mighty in battle.
10 Who is this King of glory? The LORD of Heaven's army; he is the King of glory.

Psalm 25

8 Good and upright is the LORD; therefore, he will teach sinners in his ways.
10 All the paths of the LORD are mercy and truth to those who keep his covenants and testimonies.
14 The secret of the LORD is with those who fear him, and he will show them his covenant.
15 My eyes are ever toward the LORD, for he shall save me from my enemies.

Psalm 27

1 The LORD is my light and my salvation; whom shall I fear? The LORD is the strength of my life; of whom shall I be afraid?
4 One thing have I desired of the LORD, that I may dwell in the house of the LORD all the days of my life.
11 Teach me your ways, oh LORD, and lead me in a plain path.

Psalm 28

7 The LORD is my strength and my shield; my heart trusts in him, and with my song will I praise him.
8 The LORD is the saving strength of his anointed.

Psalm 30

2 Oh LORD, my God, I cried to you, and you have healed me.
4 Sing to the LORD and give thanks at the remembrance of his holiness.
11 You have turned my mourning into dancing and surrounded me with gladness.

Psalm 31

3 You are my rock and fortress; for your name's sake lead and guide me.
14-15 I trusted in you, oh LORD. I said, You are my God. My life is in your hands; deliver me from the hand of my enemies.
23 Love the LORD, all you saints, for the LORD preserves the faithful.

Psalm 32

7 You are my hiding place; you shall preserve me from trouble; you shall surround me with songs of deliverance.
11 Be glad in the LORD and shout for joy all you who are upright in heart.

Psalm 33

1 Rejoice in the LORD, for praise is becoming of those who are upright.
2 Praise the LORD; sing to him with the your musical instruments.
3 Sing to him a new song; play skillfully with a loud noise.
4 The Word of the LORD is right, and all his works are done in truth.
5 God loves righteousness and judgment. The earth is full of the goodness of the LORD.

11 The counsel of the LORD stands forever, and his thoughts affect all generations.

12 Blessed is the nation whose God is the LORD and the people whom he has chosen for his inheritance.

18 The eye of the LORD is upon those who fear him and hope in his mercy.

Psalm 34

1 I will bless the LORD at all times; his praise shall continually be in my mouth.

2 My soul shall boast in the LORD; the humble shall hear and be glad.

4 I sought the LORD, and he heard me. He delivered me from all my fears.

7 The angel of the LORD positions himself around those who fear him and delivers them.

8 Taste and see that the LORD is good. Blessed is the man who trusts in him.

15 The eyes of the LORD are upon the righteous, and his ears are open to their cry.

16 The face of the LORD is against those who do evil.

17-18 The righteous cry, and the LORD hears and delivers them. The LORD draws close to those who are sad.

19 Many afflictions are upon the righteous, but the LORD delivers them.

22 The LORD redeems the soul of his servants, and none of those who trust in him shall be left alone.

Psalm 36

1 The wicked man says within his heart that there is no fear of God.

9 With God is the fountain of life; in his light shall we see light.

Psalm 37

3 Trust in the LORD and do good, so you may dwell in the land and be fed.

4 Delight in the LORD, and he shall give you the desires of your heart.

5 Commit your ways to the LORD; trust in him, and he shall bring it to be established.

8 Cease from anger, and reject wrath; do no evil.

13 The LORD shall laugh at him because he sees his judgment day coming.

16 A little that a righteous man has is better than the riches of many wicked men.

18 The LORD knows the days of the upright; their inheritance shall be forever.

23 The path of a good man is ordered by the LORD, and he delights in his way.

25 I have been young and now I am old; yet I have not seen the righteous

forgotten nor his children begging for bread.

28 The LORD loves judgment and does not forget his saints; they are preserved forever, but the children of the wicked shall be cut off.

34 Wait on the LORD and keep his ways, and he shall exalt you to inherit the land when the wicked are cut off.

Psalm 41

13 Blessed be the LORD God of Israel from everlasting to everlasting. Amen.

Psalm 42

2 My soul thirsts for God, for the living God. When shall I come and appear before him?

5 Why are you cast down, oh my soul? Why are you upsetting me? My hope is in God, for I shall still praise him for the help of his support.

8 The LORD will command his loving kindness in the day, and in the night his song shall be with me.

Psalm 44

6-7 I will not trust in my bow, nor shall my sword save me. But you have saved us from our enemies and have put them to shame who hated us.

8 In God we boast all the day long and praise his name forever.

Psalm 46

1 God is our refuge and strength, a very present help in trouble.

10 Be still and know that I am God; I will be exalted among the heathen. I will be exalted on the earth.

Psalm 47

7 God is the King of all the earth; sing to him praises with understanding.

Psalm 48

1 Great is the LORD and greatly to be praised in the city of our God, in the mountain of his holiness.

9 We have thought about your loving kindness, oh God, in the most sacred part of your temple.

10 According to your name, oh God, so is your praise to the ends of the earth. Your right hand is full of righteousness.

Psalm 49

5-9 Why should I fear in the days of evil? Those who trust in their wealth, none of them can redeem his brother. The redemption of their soul is precious.

16-19 Be not afraid when one is made rich, or when the glory of his house is increased. For when he dies, he shall carry nothing away; his riches shall not go with him. Even though while he lived he blessed his soul and men praised him, he shall go to the generation of his fathers, where they shall never see light.

20 Man who has honor and does not understand is like an animal that dies.

Psalm 50

16 To the wicked man God says, What have you done to declare my statutes or put my covenant in your mouth?

22 Now consider this, you who forget God. I can tear you in pieces, and there is no one who can save you.

23 Whoever offers praises glorifies me, and to him who chooses his conversation well, I will show the salvation of God.

Psalm 51

1-2 Have mercy upon me, oh God, according to your loving kindness and tender mercies. Blot out my sins. Wash me thoroughly from my sin.

5 I was formed in iniquity, and in sin did my mother conceive me.

10 Create in me a clean heart, oh God, and renew a right spirit within me. Cast me not away from your presence, and take not your Holy Spirit from me.

Psalm 53

1 The fool has said in his heart, There is no God. They are corrupt and have done abominable sins.

3 Everyone of them has gone back; they have altogether become filthy, and there is no person who does good. No, not one.

Psalm 54

4 Behold, God is my helper; the Lord is with those who uphold my soul.

7 God has delivered me out of all trouble, and my eye has seen his attention upon my enemies.

Psalm 55

17 Evening and morning will I pray and cry aloud, and he shall hear my voice.
22 Cast your burden upon the LORD, and he shall keep you; he shall never allow the righteous person to be moved.

Psalm 56

4 In God I will praise his Word. In God I have put my trust; I will not fear what man can do to me.
11 In God I put my trust; I will not be afraid what man can do to me.
12 Your vows are upon me, oh God; I will give praises to you.

Psalm 57

5 Be exalted, oh God, above the heavens; let your glory be above all the earth.
10 Your mercy is great up to the heavens and your truth up to the clouds.

Psalm 58

11 A man shall say, Certainly there is a reward for the righteous, and certainly God judges us on the earth.

Psalm 59

1 Deliver me from my enemies, oh my God; defend me from those who rise up against me.
16 I will sing of your power and your mercy in the morning, for you have been my defense and refuge in the day of my trouble.

Psalm 60

4 You have given a banner to those who fear you, that it may be displayed because of your truth.
12 Through God we shall do valiantly, for he shall tread down our enemies.

Psalm 62

2 He alone is my rock and my salvation; he is my defense. I shall not be greatly moved.
7 In God is my salvation and my glory; the rock of my strength and refuge.

Psalm 63

3 Your loving kindness is better than life, so my lips shall praise you.

Psalm 64

10 The righteous shall be glad in the LORD and shall trust in him.

Psalm 66

1 Make a joyful noise to God all the lands.
2 Sing forth the honor of his name; make his praise glorious.

Psalm 68

32 Sing to God, you kingdoms of the earth; oh, sing praises to the Lord.

Psalm 69

5 Oh God, you know my foolishness, and my sins are not hid from you.
30 I will praise the name of God with a song, and I will magnify him with thanksgiving.
33 The LORD hears the poor and does not despise his prisoners.

Psalm 71

15 My mouth shall show your righteousness and your salvation all day.
17 God, you have taught me from my youth, and I have since declared your wonderful works.
18 When I am old and grey headed, oh God, forsake me not until I have shown your strength and power to this generation.

Psalm 73

1 Truly God is good to Israel, even to those who are of a clean heart.
26 My flesh and my heart fail, but God is the strength of my heart forever.

28 It is good for me to draw near to God; I have put my trust in the Lord, so that I may declare all his works.

Psalm 75

7 God is the judge; he puts down one and sets up another.
10 All the defenses of the wicked will God cut off, but the defenses of the righteous shall be exalted.

Psalm 77

2 In the day of my trouble I sought the Lord; my wound wept in the night continually, and my soul refused to be comforted.

Psalm 80

3 Turn to us again, oh God. Cause your face to shine, and we shall be saved.

Psalm 81

9 No strange god shall be in you; neither shall you worship them.

Psalm 82

8 Arise, oh God and judge the earth, for you shall inherit all nations.

Psalm 84

2 My soul longs and faints for the presence of the LORD; my heart and my flesh cry out for the living God.
10 A day in your presence is better than a thousand. I would rather be a doorkeeper in the house of my God than to dwell in the tents of the wicked.
11 The LORD God is a sun and shield; the LORD will give grace and glory. No good thing will he withhold from those who walk upright.

Psalm 85

10-11 Mercy and truth are met together; righteousness and peace have kissed each other. Truth shall spring out of the earth, and righteousness shall look down from heaven.

Psalm 86

5 You, Lord, are good, and you are ready to forgive. You have plenty of mercy for all those who call upon you.
8 Among the gods there is none like you, oh Lord; neither are there any works like your works.

Psalm 89

2 Your mercy shall be built up forever; your faithfulness shall be established in the very heavens.
6 Who in heaven or among the sons of the mighty can be comparable to the LORD?
15 Blessed are the people who know the joyful sound; they shall walk in the light of the LORD's countenance.

Psalm 90

2 Before the mountains or earth were created, from everlasting to everlasting, you are God.
8 You have set our iniquities before yourself; our secret sins come to light in your countenance.
12 Teach us to number our days that we may apply our hearts to wisdom.

Psalm 91

1 He who dwells in the secret place of the Most High God shall abide under the shadow of the Almighty.

Psalm 92

8 You, LORD, are most high for evermore.
12, 14 The righteous shall flourish like the palm tree; they shall grow like a cedar in Lebanon. They shall still bring forth fruit in old age; they shall be fat and flourishing.
15 The LORD is upright; he is my rock, and there is no unrighteousness in him.

Psalm 93

5 Your testimonies are very sure, oh LORD; holiness becomes your house forever.

Psalm 94

22 The LORD is my defense. And my God is the rock of my refuge.

Psalm 95

1 Come, let us sing to the LORD; let us make a joyful noise to the rock of
our salvation.
2 Let us come before his presence with thanksgiving and make a joyful
noise to him with psalms.
3 The LORD is a great God and a great King above all gods.
6-7 Come, let us worship and bow down; let us kneel before the LORD
our maker. For he is our God, and we are the sheep of his pasture and the
sheep of his hand, today, if we will hear his voice.

Psalm 96

4 The LORD is great and greatly to be praised. He is to be feared above all gods.
13 The LORD is coming to judge the earth; he shall judge the world with
righteousness and the people with his truth.

Psalm 97

10 You who love the LORD, hate evil; God preserves the souls of his
saints; he delivers them out of the hand of the wicked.

Psalm 98

2 The LORD has made known his salvation; his righteousness he has
openly shown in the sight of the heathen.

Psalm 99

5 Exalt the LORD our God and worship at his footstool, for he is holy.

Psalm 100

2 Serve the LORD with gladness; come before his presence with singing.
3 Know that the LORD is God; it is he who has made us and not we
ourselves; we are his people and the sheep of his pasture.
4 Enter into his gates with thanksgiving and into his courts with praise; be
thankful to him and bless his name.

5 The LORD is good; his mercy is everlasting, and his truth endures to all generations.

Psalm 101

1 I will sing of mercy and judgment, To you, oh LORD, will I sing.

Psalm 102

11 My days are like a shadow that declines, and I wither like the grass.

Psalm 103

1 Bless the LORD, oh my soul and all that is within me. Bless his holy name.
4 God redeems your life from destruction; he crowns you with loving kindness and tender mercies.
8 The LORD is merciful and gracious; he is slow to anger and has abundant mercy.
12 As far as the east is from the west, so far has he removed our sins from us.
13 As a father pities his children, so the LORD pities those who fear him.

Psalm 104

24 Oh LORD, how magnificent are your works! In wisdom have you made them all; the earth is full of your riches.
31 The glory of the LORD shall endure forever. The LORD shall rejoice in his works.

Psalm 105

4 Seek the LORD and his strength; seek his face evermore.
8 He has remembered his covenant forever, the word which he commanded to a thousand generations.

Psalm 106

1 Praise the LORD. Give thanks to the LORD, for he is good. His mercy endures forever.

Psalm 108

5 Be exalted, oh God, above the heavens and your glory above all the earth.

Psalm 111

9 He sent redemption to his people; he has commanded his covenant forever; holy and reverent is his name.

10 The fear of the LORD is the beginning of wisdom; a good understanding have all those who do his commandments; his praise endures forever.

Psalm 112

1 Praise the LORD. Blessed is the man who fears the LORD and who delights greatly in his commandments.

4 To the upright there arises light in the darkness; he is gracious, full of compassion and righteous.

5 A good man shows favor and lends; he will guide his affairs with discretion.

7 A good man shall not be afraid of evil words; his heart is fixed, trusting in the LORD.

9 A good man has given to the poor; his righteousness endures forever. He shall be exalted with honor.

Psalm 113

3 From the rising of the sun to the going down of the sun, the LORD's name is to be praised.

4 The LORD is high above all nations and his glory above the heavens.

7 God raises up the poor out of the dust and lifts the needy out of the pit.

Psalm 115

11 You who fear the LORD, trust in the LORD; he is your help and your shield.

13 The LORD will bless those who fear him, both small and great.

16 The heavens are the LORD's, but the earth he gave to the children of men.

17-18 The dead do not praise the LORD. But we will bless the LORD from this time forth and forevermore. Praise the LORD.

Psalm 116

5 Gracious is the LORD, and righteous. Yes, our God is merciful.

6 The LORD preserves the simple. I was brought low, and he helped me.

12 What shall I give to the LORD for all his benefits toward me?

14 I will pay my vows to the LORD in the presence of all his people.

15 Precious in the sight of the LORD is the death of his saints.

Psalm 117   The shortest chapter in the *Bible*. It has 2 verses.

1 Praise the LORD, all you nations; praise him, all you people.
2 For his merciful kindness is great toward us, and the truth of the LORD endures forever. Praise the LORD.

Psalm 118   The middle chapter in the *Bible*.

1 Give thanks to the LORD, for he is good. His mercy endures forever.
6 The LORD is on my side; I will not fear. What can man do to me?
7 The LORD takes my part with those who help me; therefore, I shall see my desire upon those who hate me.
8 It is better to trust in the LORD than to put confidence in man.
14 The LORD is my strength, my song, and my salvation.
24 This is the day that the LORD has made; we will rejoice and be glad in it.
26 Blessed is he who comes in the name of the LORD.

Psalm 119   The longest chapter in the *Bible*. It has 176 verses.

2 Blessed are those who keep God's testimonies and who seek him with their whole heart.
7 I will praise God with uprightness of heart when I have learned his righteous judgments.
9 Where shall a young man cleanse his way? By taking notice according to your Word.
11 God's Word have I hid in my heart, that I might not sin against God.
18 Open my eyes, that I may behold the wonderful things out of your law.
30 I have chosen the way of truth; your judgments have I laid before me.
37 Turn my eyes away from seeing vain things. Quicken me in your ways.
45 I will walk at liberty, for I seek your thoughts.
54 Your statutes have been my songs in the house where I live.
63 I am a companion of all those who fear you and keep your commandments.
77 Let your tender mercies come to me that I may live. Your law is my delight.
90 Your faithfulness is to all generations. You have established the earth, and it remains.
99 I have more understanding than all my teachers. Your testimonies are my meditation.
130 The reading of God's Word gives light, and it gives understanding to the simple person.
140 Your Word is very pure. Therefore, your servant loves it.

160 Your Word is true from the beginning, and every one of your righteous judgments endures forever.

169 Let my cry come near before you, oh LORD. Give me understanding according to your Word.

Psalm 120

1 In my distress I cried to the LORD, and he heard me.

Psalm 121

2 My help comes from the LORD, who made heaven and earth.

3 God will not suffer your foot to be moved; he who keeps you will not slumber.

5 The LORD is your keeper and your shade upon your right hand.

8 The LORD shall preserve your going out and your coming in from this time forward, and even forevermore.

Psalm 122

1 I was glad when they said to me, Let us go into the house of the LORD.

Psalm 123

2 Behold, as the eyes of servants look to the hand of their masters, and as the eyes of a maiden looks to the hand of her mistress, so our eyes wait upon the LORD our God until he has mercy upon us.

Psalm 124

8 Our help is in the name of the LORD, who made heaven and earth.

Psalm 125

1 Those who trust in the LORD shall be like Mount Zion, which cannot be removed, but remains forever.

4 Do good, oh LORD, to those who are good and to those who are upright in their hearts.

5 As for those who turn to their crooked ways, the LORD shall lead them forward with the workers of iniquity, but peace shall be upon Israel.

Psalm 126

3 The LORD has done great things for us, and we are glad.

Psalm 127

1 Except the LORD builds the house, they labor in vain who build it; except the LORD keeps the city, the guard watches in vain.
2 It is vain for you to rise up early, to sit up late, and to eat the bread of sorrows, for God gives his loved ones sleep.
3 Children are an heritage of the LORD, and they are his reward.

Psalm 128

1 Blessed is everyone who fears the LORD and walks in his ways.

Psalm 129

4 The LORD is righteous; he has cut the safety cords of the wicked.
5 Let the wicked be confused and turned back, those who hate Jerusalem.

Psalm 130

3 If you, LORD, should count sin, who shall stand?
4 There is forgiveness with God, that he may be feared.
5 My soul waits for the LORD, and in his Word do I hope.
7 Let Israel hope in the LORD, for with the LORD there is mercy, and with him is great plenty of redemption.

Psalm 132

4-5 I will not give sleep to my eyes nor slumber to my eyelids until I find a place for the LORD, a dwelling place for the mighty God of Jacob.
13-14 The LORD has chosen Jerusalem; he has desired it for his dwelling place. This is the LORD's rest forever. Here will I dwell; it is my desire.

Psalm 133

1 Behold, how good and pleasant it is for people to dwell together in unity!

Psalm 134

2 Lift up your hands in the sanctuary and bless the LORD.

Psalm 135

3 Praise the LORD, for the LORD is good; sing praises to his name, for it is pleasant.
5 I know that the LORD is great, and that our Lord is above all gods.
6 The LORD did what he pleased in heaven and on earth and in the seas.
13 Your name, oh LORD, endures forever and throughout all generations.

Psalm 136

1 Give thanks to the LORD, for he is good. His mercy endures forever.
5-6 To him who by wisdom made the heavens, his mercy endures forever. To him who stretched out the earth above the waters, his mercy endures forever.

Psalm 138

2 I will worship toward your holy temple and praise your name for your loving kindness and for your truth. You have magnified your Word above all your name.
6 Though the LORD is high, yet he has respect for lowly people, but the proud he knows from far away.
8 The LORD will make perfect that which concerns me.

Psalm 139

1 Oh Lord, you have searched me and known me.
5 You have surrounded me from behind and before and laid your hand upon me.
7 Where shall I go from your spirit? Where shall I flee from your presence?
12 The darkness hides not from you, but the night shines as the day; the darkness and the light are both alike to you.
14 I will praise you, for I am fearfully and wonderfully made; marvellous are your works. My soul knows that well.
16 Your eyes saw me, while I was yet imperfect. In your book all my members were written, even when there was none of them.
17 How precious are your thoughts toward me, oh God! How great is the sum of them!

23-24 Search me, oh God, and know my heart; try me, and know my thoughts. See if there is any wicked way in me, and lead me in the way everlasting.

Psalm 140

1 LORD, deliver me from the evil man; preserve me from the violent man.
8 Do not grant the desires of the wicked; further not his wicked schemes because they exalt themselves.

Psalm 141

2 Let my prayer be set before you as incense and the lifting up of my hands as the evening sacrifice.
3 LORD, keep watch over my mouth; control my lips.
4 I desire my heart not to do any evil thing or to practice wicked works with men who do evil.

Psalm 143

1 Hear my prayer, oh LORD. Give ear to my words. In your faithfulness and righteousness answer me.
6 I stretch out my hands to you, oh LORD; my soul thirsts after you.
8 Cause me to hear your loving kindness in the morning, for in you do I trust. Cause me to know the way that I should walk, for I lift up my soul to you.
11 May I stand fast, oh LORD, for your name's sake; for your righteousness' sake bring my soul out of trouble.
12 By your mercy cut off my enemies and destroy all who harm my soul, for I am your servant.

Psalm 144

1 Blessed be the LORD, my strength. You teach my hands to go to war and my fingers to fight.
2 You are my goodness, my fortress, my high tower, my deliverer, my shield. In you do I trust; you subdue the people under me.

Psalm 145

3 Great is the LORD and greatly to be praised. His greatness is unsearchable.
14 The LORD upholds all who fall and raises up all who are bowed down.
17 The LORD is righteous in all his ways and holy in all his works.

19 He will fulfill the desire of those who fear him; he will hear their cry and save them.

21 My mouth shall speak the praises of the LORD. Let all flesh bless his holy name forever and ever.

Psalm 146

2 While I live will I praise the LORD; I will sing praises to my God while I have life.

6 God made heaven and earth, the sea, and all that is in them. He keeps truth forever.

Psalm 147

5 Great is our Lord and of great power; his understanding is infinite.

6 The LORD lifts up the meek; he throws the wicked down to the ground.

Psalm 149

1 Praise the LORD. Sing to the LORD a new song and give him praise in the congregation of the saints.

3 Let us praise his name with dancing; let us sing praises to him with musical instruments.

4 The LORD takes pleasure in his people; he will beautify the meek with salvation.

5 Let the saints be joyful in glory; let them sing aloud while lying on their beds.

Psalm 150

2 Praise the LORD for his mighty acts; praise him according to his excellent greatness.

6 Let every thing that has breath praise the LORD. Praise you the LORD.

Proverbs

The book of Proverbs contains the wisdom of God for us. He instructs those who choose to follow him in the ways that please him. Ponder what God is saying to you. Proverbs contains very practical advice. It is wisdom that guides us to live godly lives that are pleasing to God.

Proverbs 1

5 A wise man will hear and increase learning. A man of understanding will get wise counsel.

7 The fear of the LORD is the beginning of knowledge, but fools despise wisdom and instruction.

8 Hear the instruction of your father, and do not reject the law of your mother.

Proverbs 2

6 The LORD gives wisdom; out of his mouth comes knowledge and understanding.

11 Good choices shall preserve you; understanding shall keep you.

20 Walk in the paths of good men and protect the ways of the righteous.

Proverbs 3

1-2 Many days, long life and peace shall be yours for obeying my commandments.

6 In all your ways acknowledge God, and he will direct your paths.

9 Honor the LORD with your possessions and with the first of your profits.

11-12 Do not despise and grow weary of the correction of the LORD. Whom the LORD loves he corrects.

14 Wisdom is better than silver, and the gain more than fine gold.

18 Wisdom is a tree of life to those who take hold of her.

26 The LORD shall be your strength and shall keep your foot from being moved.

33 The curse of the LORD is in the house of the wicked, but he blesses the dwelling of the just.

Proverbs 4

1 Children, hear the instruction of your father and get to know understanding.

5 Get wisdom, get understanding; do not shy from the words of God's mouth.

7 Wisdom is the principal thing, so get wisdom, and then get understanding.

8 Exalt wisdom and she shall promote you; wisdom shall bring you to honor, so embrace her.

23 Keep your heart pure, for out of it come the values of your life.

Proverbs 5

3-4 The lips of a strange woman drip like a honeycomb, and her mouth is smoother than oil, but her goal is bitter and sharp as a two-edged sword.

15 Drink water out of your own vessel and running waters out of your own well.

18-19 Let your fountain be blessed and rejoice with the wife of your youth. Let her full body be pleasing to you; let her breasts satisfy you at all times, and be excited always with her love.

21 The ways of man do not escape the eyes of the LORD; he knows them all.

23 Man shall die without instruction, and in the greatness of his foolishness he shall go astray.

Proverbs 6

6 See the ant, you who are lazy; consider the ant's work and be wise.

16-19 These seven things the LORD hates; they are an abomination to him: A proud look, a lying tongue, hands who shed innocent blood, a heart that devises wicked ideas, feet that are swift in running to mischief, a false witness who speaks lies, and he who sows discord among friends.

29 If you commit adultery with your neighbor's wife, then whoever touches her shall not be innocent.

32 He who commits adultery with a woman lacks understanding and destroys his own soul.

Proverbs 8

5 You who are simple and are fools, understand wisdom and develop an understanding heart.

8 All the words from God's mouth are in righteousness; there is nothing wrong or unreasonable in them.

11 Wisdom is better than rubies, and nothing compares to it.

13 The fear of the LORD is to hate what he hates: evil and its ways, pride, arrogance, and a foul mouth.

22 The LORD knew me in the beginning of his ways before his creation.

Proverbs 9

10 The fear of the LORD is the beginning of wisdom, and the knowledge of that which is holy is understanding.

Proverbs 10

2 Treasures of wickedness profit nothing, but righteousness delivers from death.

3 The LORD will not allow the soul of the righteous man to hunger, but he throws away the important things of the wicked.

9 He who walks with integrity is sure of himself, but the man who is corrupt shall be found out.

10 He who fools you by his eye causes sorrow, but an incompetent person shall fall.

17 He who is leading a good life keeps instruction, but he who refuses correction is doing wrong.

21 The lips of the righteous feed many, but fools die for want of wisdom.

25 As the whirlwind passes, so does the wicked, but the righteous man has an everlasting foundation.

27 The fear of the LORD prolongs life, but the years of the wicked shall be shortened.

Proverbs 11

2 When pride comes, then comes shame, but with the meek is wisdom.

3 The integrity of the good man shall guide them, but the unreasonableness of sinners shall destroy them.

4 Riches profit nothing in the day of God's judgment, but righteousness delivers you from death.

7 When a wicked man dies, his hope shall perish.

11 By the blessing of upright people the city is exalted.

14 Where no counsel is, the people fall, but in the multitude of counselors there is safety.

15 He who would be a guarantee for a stranger shall get hurt.

17 The merciful man does good to his own soul, but he who is cruel troubles his own family.

18 The wicked are deceitful, but he who sows righteousness reaps a sure reward.

19 As righteousness relates to good life, so he who pursues evil pursues it to his own death.

23 The desire of the righteous person is only for good, but the wicked person can only expect wrath.

24 He who gives cheerfully will be blessed; he who does not give cheerfully may lose what he has.

27 He who enjoys being good receives favor, but he who seeks to do harm, it shall come to him.

28 He who trusts in his riches shall fall, but the righteous shall flourish.

29 He who troubles his own house shall inherit the wind, and the fool shall be servant to the wise of heart.

30 The fruit of the righteous is a tree of life, and he who wins souls is wise.

Proverbs 12

1 He who loves instruction loves knowledge, but he who hates correction is stubborn.

2 A good man obtains favor of the LORD, but a man of wicked intent the LORD will condemn.

4 A virtuous woman is a crown to her husband, but she who makes him ashamed destroys the man.

8 A man shall be praised according to his wisdom, but he who is of a wicked heart shall be despised.

11 He who tills his land shall be satisfied with bread, but he who follows arrogant persons is void of understanding.

13 The wicked is caught by the evil of his lips, but the just shall come out of trouble.

14 A man shall be satisfied with good by the goodness of his mouth.

16 A fool's wrath is well known, but a thoughtful man covers his shame.

17 He who speaks truth shows forth righteousness, but a false witness is deceitful.

18 He who does not choose his words carefully can cut another like a sword, but the tongue of the wise heals.

19 Truth shall be established forever, but a lying tongue is but for a moment.

24 The hand of the diligent shall govern, but the slothful shall be under condemnation.

26 The righteous man is more excellent than his neighbor, but the way of the wicked tempts them.

27 The lazy man does not cook what he killed while hunting, but the man who cares is valuable.

Proverbs 13

1 A wise son hears his father's advice, but a critical son rejects correction.

3 He who controls his mouth keeps his life, but he who opens it wide shall be destroyed.

4 The soul of the lazy person desires much but has nothing; the soul of the persistent person shall be made full.

7 He who makes himself rich may have nothing; he who makes himself poor may get great riches.

11 Wealth gotten by pride shall be diminished, but he who gathers by labor shall increase.

12 Hope deferred makes the heart sick, but when the desire comes, it is a tree of life.

16 Every wise man deals with knowledge, but a fool lays open his folly.

20 He who walks with wise men shall be wise, but a companion of fools shall be destroyed.

22 A good man leaves an inheritance to his children's children, and the wealth of the sinner is laid up for the just.

24 He who spares the rod hates his son, but he who loves his son corrects him on time.

Proverbs 14

2 He who walks in his uprightness fears the LORD, but he who is crooked in his ways despises him.

5 A faithful witness will not lie, but a false witness will speak lies.

6 A scorner seeks wisdom and does not find it, but knowledge is easy to him who understands.

14 The backslider in heart shall be filled with his own ways, and a good man shall be satisfied with himself.

15 The simple believes every word, but the thoughtful man considers his path.

16 A wise man fears and departs from evil, but the fool over reacts with confidence.

17 He who is soon angry deals foolishly; a man of wicked actions is hated.

22 Those who devise evil do error, but mercy and truth come to those who seek to do good.

23 In all labor there is profit, but only talk leads towStoneard poverty.

27 The fear of the LORD is a fountain of life.

29 He who is slow to wrath is of great understanding, but he who is hasty exalts folly.

31 He who oppresses the poor angers his Maker, but he who honors the LORD has mercy on the poor.

34 Righteousness exalts a nation, but sin is a reproach to any person.

Proverbs 15

1 A soft answer turns away wrath, but bitter words stir up anger.

3 The eyes of the LORD are in every place, seeing the evil and the good.

5 A fool despises his father's instruction, but he who respects correction is wise.

11 Hell and destruction are before the LORD; how much more does he know the hearts of people?

14 The heart of him who has understanding seeks knowledge, but the mouth of fools feeds on foolishness.

16 Better it is to have little with the fear of the LORD than to have great treasure and trouble.

18 An angry man stirs up strife, but he who is slow to anger appeases strife.

28 The heart of the righteous studies before answering, but the mouth of the wicked pours out evil things.

29 The LORD is far from the wicked, but he hears the prayer of the righteous.

32 He who refuses instruction despises his own soul, but he who hears correction gets understanding.

Proverbs 16

2 All the ways of a man are clean in his own eyes, but the LORD weighs the spirit within him.

3 Commit your works to the LORD, and your thoughts shall be established.

11 A just balance scale is the LORD's measure.

18 Pride goes before destruction and a haughty spirit before a fall.

20 He who handles a matter wisely shall find good, and he who trusts in the LORD is happy.

29 A violent man tries to fool his neighbor and leads him away from good.

Proverbs 17

3 The LORD tests the hearts of people.

6 Children's children are the reward of old men, and the glory of children are their fathers.

9 He who covers a sin seeks his own approval, but he who repeats sin separates friends.

13 If one rewards evil as being good, evil shall not depart from his house.

16 A fool tries to buy wisdom when he lacks it.

17 A friend loves you at all times, and a brother is born to help you.

19 He who loves manipulating actually loves strife, and he who exalts himself seeks destruction.

21 He who gets a fool does it to his sorrow, and the father of a fool has no joy.

22 A merry heart does good like a medicine, but a broken spirit dries the bones.

27 He who has knowledge spares his words, and a man of understanding has an excellent spirit within himself.

28 Even a fool, when he holds his emotions, is counted wise. He who shuts his lips is a man of understanding.

Proverbs 18

1 A man who desires to isolate himself may seek to manipulate wisdom.

3 When the wicked man comes, then comes contempt and disgrace.

10 The name of the LORD is a strong tower; the righteous run into it and are safe.

12 Before destruction the heart of man is haughty, and before honor is humility.

13 He who answers a matter before he hears it is foolish. It may prove shameful to him.

15 The heart of a thoughtful person gets knowledge, and the ear of the wise seeks knowledge.

16 A man's gift makes room for him and brings him before great men.

17 He who is first in his own cause seems just, but his neighbor comes and questions him.

18 Picking by chance can cause differences to cease, even with the mighty.

19 A brother who is offended is harder to win than a strong city.

21 Death and life are in the power of the tongue, and those who love it shall eat the fruit of it.

22 Whoever finds a wife finds a good thing and is blessed by the LORD.

24 A man who has friends must show himself friendly, and there is a friend who sticks closer than a brother.

Proverbs 19

1 Better is the poor man who walks with integrity, than he who is unreasonable when he talks and is a fool.

3 The foolishness of man alters his way, and his heart is anxious against the LORD.

4 Wealth makes many friends, but the poor is separated from his neighbor.

9 A false witness shall not go unpunished, and he who speaks lies shall perish.

13 A foolish son is not the joy of his father, and an arguing wife is annoying.

14 Houses and riches are the inheritance of fathers, and a wise wife is from the LORD.

17 He who has pity upon the poor lends to the LORD, and he who does so will be blessed by the LORD.

18 Correct your son while there is hope, and let not your soul spare him from crying.

19 A man of great wrath shall suffer punishment, but if you save him, you will have to punish him again.

20 Hear counsel and receive instruction, so that you may be wise when you are older.

21 There are many plans in a man's heart; nevertheless, the will of the LORD shall prevail.

22 The path of a man is his kindness, and a poor man is better than a liar.

23 The fear of the LORD ends in life, and he who has it shall be satisfied and avoid evil.

25 Strike a complaining person, and the simple person will beware.

26 He who degrades his father and chases away his mother is a son who causes shame and brings dishonor.

27 Stop listening to instructions that cause you to stray from words of knowledge.

29 Judgments are prepared for degrading people and whip lashes for the back of fools.

Proverbs 20

1 Wine is a mocker; strong drink causes aggressive behavior, and whoever is deceived by it is not wise.

3 It is an honor for a man to cease from strife, but every fool will be interfering.

4 The lazy man who will not plow if it is cold will beg at harvest and have nothing.

6 Most men will brag how good they are, but a faithful man is hard to find.

7 The just man walks with integrity, and his children become blessed.

10 Dishonest weights and measures are an abomination to the LORD.

11 Even a child is known by what he does, whether his work is pure and right.

12 The hearing ear and the seeing eye, the LORD has made them both.

13 Do not love to sleep; it may lead to poverty. Wake up and obtain bread.

15 There are many rubies and abundant gold, but the lips of knowledge are precious jewels.

17 The bread of deceit is sweet to a man, but afterwards his mouth shall be filled with gravel.

18 Every good plan is established by counsel; do not make war without good advice.

19 He who goes about with a loose mouth reveals secrets; therefore, do not make friends with a person who loves to flatter you.

20 He who curses his father or mother, his importance shall fail him.

21 An inheritance may be gotten hastily, but it may not become a blessing.

22 Do not say you will avenge evil, but wait on the LORD to save you.

24 Life's path of mankind is of the LORD; how can a man then understand his own way?

25 A man is trapped who outwardly appears to be holy and yet vows to commit sin.

27 The spirit of man is light to the LORD; the light reveals man's inner secrets to the LORD.

29 The glory of young men is their strength, and the beauty of old men is their grey head.

Proverbs 21

2 A man's actions are right in his own eyes, but the LORD looks at his heart.

3 To do justly with good judgment is more acceptable to the LORD than good works.

5 Your thoughts of caring tend to result in plenty, but those who are hasty tend to still want.

7 Taking what is not theirs shall destroy them because they refuse to be accountable.

8 The ways of a guilty man are crooked and strange, but as for the man who is pure, his work is right.

9 It is better to stay in your farthest room than with a fighting woman.

10 The soul of the wicked man desires to do evil; his neighbor is not safe from his eyes.

12 The righteous man wisely avoids dwelling with the wicked because God overthrows those who are bad.

13 Whoever plugs his ears at the cry of the poor will cry himself and not be heard.

14 A gift given in secret may satisfy anger, and a reward given may avoid strong wrath.

15 It is joy to the just person to do justice, but destruction shall come to those who do evil.

16 The man who wanders away from understanding shall remain in the company of the dead.

17 He who loves pleasure shall be a poor man; he who loves wine and money shall not be satisfied.

19 It is better to live in the wilderness than with an arguing angry woman.

20 There is wealth and luxury in the house of the wise, but a foolish man wastes it.

21 He who follows after righteousness and mercy finds life, righteousness, and honor.

23 Whoever controls his tongue keeps his soul from trouble.

24 Proud arrogant scorner is his name; he enjoys being mean.

25 The desire for being lazy kills him, for he refuses to work.

26 He covets and is greedy all day long, but the righteous gives and gives.

27 The sacrifice of sinners is an abomination; how much more when he brings it with a wicked mind?

28 A false witness has no value, but the true witness shall be heard.

29 A wicked man hardens his face, but the upright determines his own way.

30 There is no wisdom, understanding, or counsel against the LORD.

31 The horse is prepared for the day of battle, but safety is of the LORD.

Proverbs 22

1 Having a good name is to be chosen over great riches, and loving favor over silver and gold.

2 The rich and poor meet together; the LORD is the maker of them all.

4 By humility and fear of the LORD comes riches, honor, and life.

5 Thorns and traps are in the way of the crooked man; he who keeps his soul shall stay far from them.

6 Train up a child in the way he should go, and when he is old, he will not depart from it.

8 He who sows evil shall reap pride, and the rod of his anger shall fail him.

9 He who has a giving eye shall be blessed because he gives of his bread to the poor.

10 Cast out the negative person, and division shall leave.

12 The eyes of the LORD preserve knowledge, and he overthrows the words of evil people.

14 Talking with immoral women leads to a deep pit; he who is hated by the LORD shall fall in that same pit.

15 Foolishness is part of the heart of a child, but the rod of correction shall drive it far from him.

22 Rob not the poor because he is poor; neither oppress the afflicted.

24-25 Make no friendship with an angry man, and do not go with a mad man. Do not learn his ways; it will trap your soul.

28 Do not remove historical landmarks which your fathers have set.

Proverbs 23

4 Do not labor to be rich; cease from your own wisdom.

9 Do not speak in the ears of a fool, for he will despise your wisdom.

13 Do not withhold correction from the child because if you beat him with the rod, he shall not die.

17 Let not your heart envy sinners, but be in the fear of the LORD always.

20-21 Do not be among alcohol drinkers, for the drunkard shall come to poverty; their drowsiness from drinking shall clothe them with rags.

22 Pay attention to your father, and despise not your mother when she is old.

23 Buy the truth, and do not sell it. Buy wisdom, instruction, and understanding.

24-25 The father of the righteous shall greatly rejoice, and he who gets a wise child shall have joy. Your father and mother shall be glad in you.

29-30 Those who sip wine and drink mixed drinks are associated with trouble, sorrow, fights, and bloodshot eyes.

31-32 Look not upon wine when it is red, when its color and movement interest you. In the end, it will bite and sting you like poison.

Proverbs 24

1-2 Do not be envious of evil men, nor desire to be with them. Their heart studies destruction, and their lips talk of mischief.

5 A wise man is strong; he increases in strength.

17-18 Do not rejoice when your enemy falls; when the LORD sees that, it displeases him, and he may turn away his wrath from your enemy.

20 There shall be no reward for the evil man; the light of the wicked shall be put out.

23 Be wise; it is not good to have respect for guilty persons in judgment.

28 Do not witness against your neighbor without cause, and deceive not with your speech.

Proverbs 25

7-8 It is better if you are asked by the host to be the guest of honor than to be just one person in the crowd. Allow it to happen naturally; do not let your neighbor embarrass you in any way.

9-10 Discuss your viewpoint privately with your neighbor, so it remains a private matter and will not be heard publicly and possibly shame you.

14 Whoever boasts falsely of himself is like clouds and wind without rain.

18 A man who tells lies against his neighbor hurts him deeply.

19 Having confidence in an unfaithful man while you are in trouble is like a broken tooth and an injured foot.

20 Singing happy songs to a sad person may be like taking away his warm coat in cold weather.

21-22 If your enemy is hungry, give him bread to eat. If he is thirsty, give him water, for you shall heap coals of fire upon his head, and the LORD shall reward you.

25 Good news from a far country is like cold water to a thirsty person.

28 He who does not rule over his own spirit is like a ghetto in the city.

Proverbs 26

4 Do not answer a fool's foolishness; you may prove to be like him.

8 He who glues a stone to a sling shot is foolish; so is he who gives honor to a fool.

11 As a dog returns to his vomit, so a fool returns to his folly.

16 The lazy person thinks he is wiser in his own conceit than seven men who can give him good reasons.

20 Where there is no wood, the fire goes out. Where there is no gossiper, the conflict ceases.

21 As coals are to burning coals and wood is to fire, so it is with a contentious man to kindle strife.

24 He who hates, tears apart with his speech and lays up deceit to himself.

Proverbs 27

2 Let another man praise you; do not do it with your own mouth.

4 Wrath is cruel and anger is outrageous, but who is able to withstand envy?

6 Faithful are the wounds of a friend, but the kisses of an enemy are deceitful.

9 Perfume rejoices the heart; so does a man's friend who gives wise counsel.

15 Continual dripping on a rainy day and an arguing woman are alike.

17 As iron sharpens iron, so a man sharpens the disposition of his friend.

18 Whoever trims the fig tree shall eat of its fruit. He who serves his master shall be honored.

Proverbs 28

1 The wicked flee when no man chases, but the righteous are bold as a lion.

2 There are many leaders of sinful nations, but by a man of understanding and knowledge, his nation shall stand.

4 Those who reject the law praise the wicked, but those who keep the law fight against them.

5 Evil men do not understand judgment, but those who seek the LORD understand all things.

6 Better is the poor man who walks with integrity than he who is dishonest and rich.

7 Whoever keeps the law is a wise son, but he who is a companion of evil men shames his father.

8 He who lends at high interest for unjust gain increases his wealth, but he unknowingly gathers it for another who is wiser, who will pity the poor.

9 He who does not abide by the law, even his prayers shall go unanswered.

11 The rich man is wise in his own pride, but the poor man who has understanding searches him out.

12 When righteous men rejoice, there is great glory, but when the wicked have power, men prefer to hide.

13 He who covers his sins shall not prosper, but whoever confesses and rejects them shall have mercy.

14 Happy is the man who is fearful, but he who hardens his heart shall fall into trouble.

17 A man who is violent and draws blood of any person shall flee to the pit; let no man save him.

20 A faithful man shall have great blessings, but he who is quick to get rich shall not be innocent.

22 He who has to be rich has an evil eye and considers not that poverty shall come upon him.

24 Whoever robs his father or mother and says, It is not wrong; the same is the friend of destruction.

25 He who has a proud heart stirs up division, but he who puts his trust in the LORD shall be filled.

27 He who gives to the poor shall not have wants, but he who hides his eyes to the poor shall be cursed.

Proverbs 29

6 There is a trap that waits the evil man who sins, but the righteous sing and rejoice.

7 The righteous person considers the needs of the poor, but the wicked deny their needs.

11 A fool speaks his mind, but a wise man gives thought to his words.

16 When the wicked are multiplied, transgression increases, but the righteous shall see their fall.

26 Many seek the ruler's favor, but every man's judgment comes from the LORD.

Proverbs 30

5 Every Word of God is true; he shields those who put their trust in him.

6 Add not to God's words, or he may correct you, and you may be found to be a liar.

20 This is the way of an adulterous woman: she eats, wipes her mouth, and says, I have done no wickedness.

32 If you have done foolishly in lifting up yourself, or if you have thought evil, lay your hand over your mouth.

Proverbs 31

8 Speak up for the mentally challenged, so many do not destroy them.

10-12, 25 Who can find a virtuous wife? Her price is far above rubies. The heart of her husband trusts her. She will do him good and not evil all the days of her life. Strength and honor are her clothes.

26, 28 A virtuous wife opens her mouth with wisdom, and her tongue is the law of kindness. Her children call her blessed; her husband praises her.

30 Favor is deceitful, and beauty is vain, but a woman who fears the LORD shall be praised.

Ecclesiastes

King Solomon wrote Ecclesiastes and was extremely wise. He was an old man when he wrote about his perceptions on life. This is well worth studying because it is so thought provoking.

Ecclesiastes 1

9 Past history reflects what future history will be; there is nothing new under the sun.

Ecclesiastes 2

14 The wise man's eyes are in his head, but the fool walks in darkness.

24 There is nothing better for a man than something to eat and drink. He should enjoy his labor that is from the hand of God.

Ecclesiastes 3

1 To everything there is a season and a time for every purpose.

2 There is a time to be born, a time to die, a time to plant, and a time to harvest.

3 There is a time to kill, a time to heal, a time to tear down, and a time to build up.

4 There is a time to weep, a time to laugh, a time to mourn, and a time to dance.

5 There is a time to throw stones away, a time to gather stones together, a time to embrace, and a time not to embrace.

6 There is a time to receive, a time to lose, a time to keep, and a time to discard.

7 There is a time to tear apart, a time to sew, a time to keep silent, and a time to speak.

8 There is a time to love, a time to hate, a time of war, and a time of peace.

11 God has made everything beautiful in his time; he has put time in man's

heart, so that no man can discover God's plans from their beginnings to the end.

13 Every man should eat, drink, and enjoy the fruits of his labor. It is the gift of God.

14 Whatever God does, it shall be forever; nothing can add or subtract from it. God does it, so men should greatly respect him.

Ecclesiastes 4

9 Two are better than one because they receive a good reward for their labor.

12 If one man can prevail against one other, two shall withstand one. A three stranded cord is not easily broken.

Ecclesiastes 5

1 Stand upright when you go into the house of God. Be ready to receive and hear God. If you do not pay attention, you will do evil.

4 When you make a vow to God, do not delay doing it, for God has no pleasure in fools; do as you have vowed.

7 In many dreams and many words there come many selfish plans, but learn to follow God.

10 He who loves silver shall not be satisfied, nor he who loves great profit. This leads to self-centeredness.

12 Sleep to a working man is sweet, whether he eats little or much, but seeking to be rich will not allow him to sleep well.

Ecclesiastes 7

1 Having a good name is better than precious oil.

8 Better is the end of something than the beginning of it. To be patient in spirit is better than to be proud.

9 Do not be angry, for anger dwells in fools.

13 Consider the works of God. Who can make straight what God has made crooked?

14 In the day of prosperity be joyful, but in the day of trials consider who God has set one over the other.

19 Wisdom strengthens the wise more than ten mighty men.

20 There is not a just man upon earth who does good and sins not.

21 Do not hear all the words that are spoken; you may hear your helper curse you.

24 Consider that which is far off and exceeding deep; who can detect it?

26 More bitter than death is the woman who sets traps; whoever pleases

God shall escape her, but the sinner shall be caught by her.

29 I found that God has made man upright, but man has sought to follow his own path.

Ecclesiastes 8

6 With every purpose there is time and judgment; therefore, the misery of man is great upon him.

11 Because the judgment against an evil work is not executed speedily, the hearts of the sons of men are fully set to do evil.

12 Though a sinner does evil a hundred times and lives long, yet know that it shall be well with those who fear God.

14 Boasting is done upon the earth that there are good men who seem to be wicked, and there are wicked men who seem to be good. This often leads men to be self-admired.

Ecclesiastes 9

11 I observe that the race is not always won by the swift, nor the battle won by the strong. The wise may go without bread. Riches do not go to wise men, nor winning to men of skill, but time and chance happen to them all.

18 Wisdom is better than weapons of war, but one sinner can destroy much good.

Ecclesiastes 10

2 A wise man's heart is in his right hand, but a fool's heart is in his left; they are opposites of one another.

3 When he who is a fool walks around, his wisdom fails him, and he un-knowingly says to everyone that he is a fool.

12 The words of a wise man's mouth are gracious, but the lips of a fool will quickly consume himself.

13 The beginning of the words of his mouth is foolishness, and the end of his talk is mischievous madness.

Ecclesiastes 11

7 Light is beneficial and pleasant; it is for the eyes to see what the sun gives light to.

8 If a man lives many years, let him remember the days of darkness, for there shall be many.

9 Rejoice young men in your youth, and let your heart cheer you in those

days. Walk in the ways of your heart, but know that for all these things God will bring you into judgment.

Ecclesiastes 12

1 Remember now your Creator in the days of your youth, while the evil days do not come or your life draws to a close.
7 Remember your Creator when your dust returns to the earth as it was and your spirit returns to God who gave it.
13-14 Hear the conclusion to the whole matter: Fear God and keep his commandments, for this is the whole duty of man. God shall bring man's every work into judgment, including every secret thing, whether it was good or evil.

Song of Solomon

This book is a love story that depicts the ideal love of a man and his wife. It also depicts the love of God for his bride. God's bride is the people of faith who make up Christ's church on earth. This marriage is a future event.

The whole book is one that needs spiritual discernment for understanding.

Song of Solomon 2

4 He brought me to his banqueting table, and his banner over me was love.
16 My beloved is mine, and I am his. He feeds his flock among the lilies.

Song of Solomon 8

6 Set me as a seal upon your heart, for love is strong as death; jealousy is cruel as the grave.
7 Floods cannot stop love. If a man gives all his possessions for love, it still would not stop it.

Isaiah

Isaiah is a prophetic book. It contains strong proof that God alone is Jesus Christ. It identifies God as man's only Savior, Redeemer, Creator and Judge. It is Christ who fulfills these prophecies and the historical settings stated.

Isaiah 9 gives us the birth of Christ. It states that he is the Mighty God. In a number of other chapters, God says that he alone is God. This is not a conflict when you understand the meaning of absolute holiness. Jesus, our Emmanuel, has to be very God. It is verified in the book of Titus, too. Simply stated, if Christ were anything minutely less than God himself, he would not be holy enough for God to use Christ to redeem man from his sin.

In Isaiah 7 you see the use of the word Emmanuel. It means Christ is God with us. Isaiah states that God cannot contradict his Word. Isaiah 26 says, Trust in the Lord always. God could not say this if his Word were to contain any unreliable information. If his Word were not all truth, how could he instruct us to search the Word of the Lord as he does in Isaiah 34?

In Isaiah, when using the words "alone" or "only" God affirms the "us"and "our" in Genesis 1:26-27 and Genesis 3:22. The "us" and "our" refer to God and Christ, equally. The *Holy Bible* is the most important book in the world.

Isaiah 1

17 Learn to do well. Seek justice, relieve the oppressed, judge the fatherless, and plead for the widow.
18 Come now, and let us reason together, says the LORD; though your sins be as scarlet, they shall be white as snow.
19 If you are willing and obedient, you shall eat good food from the land.

Isaiah 2

11 Arrogant men shall be humbled and bowed down; the LORD alone shall be exalted on judgment day.
12, 19 That day, the day of the second coming of the LORD, the LORD of hosts shall come upon everyone who is proud and lofty, and those men shall be brought down. Those men shall go into the caves of the earth for fear of the LORD when he violently shakes the earth.

Isaiah 3

10 Say to the righteous, It shall be well with you, for they shall eat the results of what they do.
11 Warn the wicked! It shall not be good for them, because the reward of their bad deeds shall be given back to them.

Isaiah 5

16 The LORD of hosts shall be exalted in judgment because he is holy; he shall be sanctified in righteousness.
20 Warn those who call evil good and good evil; they prefer darkness over light!
21 Warn those who think they are wise in their own eyes and so clever!
22 Warn those who drink strong mixed drinks and boast about it.

Isaiah 6

3 One angel cried to another, Holy, holy, holy is the LORD of hosts; the whole earth is full of his glory.
5 Then I said, sadly crying, I am worthless; I am a man of unclean lips, and I live with people of unclean lips, for my eyes have seen the King, the LORD of hosts.
8 I heard the voice of the Lord, saying, Whom shall I send, and who will go for us (Christ and God)? Then I said, Here am I; send me.

Isaiah 7

14 Therefore, the Lord himself shall give you a sign. Behold, a virgin shall conceive and bear a son, and she shall call his name Emmanuel. (Again, this means, God with us. See the book of Matthew, also.)

Isaiah 8

13 Sanctify the LORD of hosts, and let him be your fear, for he will be your judge.
16 Bind up God's testimony; seal the law among my disciples.
20 If they speak not according to the law and to the testimony, it is because there is no light in them.

Isaiah 9

2 The people who walked in darkness have seen a great light; those who dwell in the land of the shadow of death, upon them has the light shined.
6 To us a child is born, to us a son is given, and the government shall be upon his shoulder. His name shall be called Wonderful, Counselor, The mighty God, The everlasting Father, The Prince of Peace.
7 Of the increase of his government and peace, there shall be no end upon the throne of David and upon his kingdom, to order it and to establish it

with judgment and with justice from now on, even forever. The zeal of the LORD of hosts will perform this.

Isaiah 12

2 Behold, God is my salvation; I will trust and not be afraid, for the LORD JEHOVAH is my strength and my song. He is my salvation.
5 Sing to the LORD, for he has done excellent things that are known throughout all the earth.

Isaiah 25

4 God has been the strength to poor and needy people; he is their refuge from the storms of life.
8 He will swallow up death in victory, and the Lord GOD will wipe away all their tears from their eyes, for the LORD has spoken it.

Isaiah 26

4 Trust in the LORD forever, for in the LORD JEHOVAH is everlasting strength.
21 Behold, the LORD comes out of his place to punish the peoples of the earth for their sins.

Isaiah 29

13 The Lord said, By the measure of their spoken words do these people honor me.
15 Woe to those who seek to hide from the LORD. They live their lives in secret, saying, Who can see us now or knows us?
16 Surely your turning of things upside down shall be similar to the potter and his clay. Shall the work say of him who made it, He made me not?
18 In the Day of the Lord, the deaf shall hear the words of the book, and the eyes of the blind shall see out of darkness.

Isaiah 33

5 The LORD is exalted, for he dwells on high; he has filled Zion (Jerusalem) with judgment and righteousness.
6 Wisdom and knowledge shall be the stability of your present life; the fear of the LORD is your treasure.

20 Look upon Zion, and see Jerusalem as a quiet habitation, a tabernacle that shall not be taken down.

21 It is in Jerusalem that the glorious LORD will be to us as a place of wide rivers and streams.

Isaiah 34

16 Seek out of the book of the LORD and read it; not one written thing shall fail.

Isaiah 35

4-7 Say to those who are fearful, Be strong, fear not; behold, your God will come with vengeance. He will come and save you. Then the eyes of the blind shall open, and the ears of the deaf shall hear. Then shall the lame man leap, and the tongue of the deaf shall sing. And the dry ground shall become a pool, and the thirsty land shall become springs of water.

10 The ransomed of the LORD shall return and come to Zion with songs and everlasting joy upon their heads, for sorrow and sighing shall flee away.

Isaiah 37

16 Oh LORD of hosts, God of Israel, who dwells between the angels, you are the God, only you alone. You have made heaven and earth.

Isaiah 40

10 Behold, the Lord GOD will come with power, and his arm shall rule for him; behold, his reward is with him, and his plans are set before him.

18 To whom will you liken God, or to what likeness will you compare him?

28 Have you not known or heard that the everlasting God, the LORD, the Creator of all the earth, sleeps not? Neither does he grow weary. You cannot begin to comprehend God.

31 Those who wait upon the LORD shall renew their strength; they shall mount up with wings as eagles; they shall run and not be weary. They shall walk and not faint.

Isaiah 41

4 Who has thought and done it, calling the generations from the beginning? I the LORD, the first and the last; I am he who has the foreknowledge.

10 Fear not, for I am with you; be not dismayed, for I am your God; I will

strengthen you and help you. I will uphold you with the right hand of my righteousness.

14 Fear not, I will help you, says the LORD, your Redeemer, the Holy One of Israel.

Isaiah 42

5 God created the heavenlies and stretched them out; he created the earth and that which comes out of it; he gives breath to the people who walk upon it and the spirit who lives within them.

8 I am the LORD; that is my name. My glory I will not give to another nor give it to man's idols.

9 Take notice, the words I spoke came to be, and the new words I declare before they happen will also come to be.

12 Let the people give glory to the LORD and declare his praise to the islands.

17 Those people shall be turned back; they shall be greatly ashamed who trust in man made images as gods.

Isaiah 43

3 I am the LORD your God, the Holy One of Israel, your Savior.

10 You are my witnesses, says the LORD, and my servant whom I have chosen that you may know, believe and understand that I am he. Before me there was no God formed, neither shall there be after me.

11 I, even I, am the LORD, and beside me there is no savior.

12 I have declared, I have saved, and I have shown, when there was no strange god among you; therefore, you are my witnesses, says the LORD, that I am God.

13 Yes, before the creation was, I am he, and there is none who can take away from me.

25 I, even I, am he who erases your sins for my own sake, and I promise not to remember them.

Isaiah 44

6-7 The LORD says, I am the first, and I am the last; beside me there is no God. And who is there like me who shall create their plan, declare it, and set it in order?

8 Fear not; neither be afraid. Is there a God beside me? No, there is no other God.

9 People who make man-made idols work in vain; they will be ashamed.

10 Who has formed a god or idol that is profitable?

24 The LORD, your Redeemer, who formed you from the womb, says, I am the LORD who makes all things, who stretches out the heavens alone and spreads abroad the earth by myself.

25 Creation knowledge frustrates liars.

Isaiah 45

5-6 I am the LORD, and there is none else; there is no God beside me. I have provided for you though you have not known me, so all may always know that there is none beside me. I am the LORD, and there is none else.

14 The LORD says, Foreigners shall come to you, Israel, recognizing you have God. They shall plead saying, surely God is in you, and there is none else.

15 God works in mysterious ways; he is the God and Savior of Israel.

17 Israel will be saved by the LORD with an everlasting salvation; Israel will never be put to shame or disgraced.

18 God himself formed the earth; he established it for good reason. He formed it to be inhabited. God says, I am the LORD, and there is none else.

19 I have not spoken in secret. You do not seek me in vain; I the LORD speak righteousness; I declare things that are true.

20 Assemble yourselves together. Other nations that set up idols and pray to a god who cannot save have no knowledge.

21 I am the LORD, and there is no God apart from me. I am a righteous God and a Savior; there is none but me.

22 Everyone, look to me and be saved, for I am God, and there is none else.

23 I have sworn by myself. My Word has gone out of my mouth in righteousness, and it is true. To me every knee shall bow and every tongue shall confess.

24 Surely confess, In the LORD I have righteousness and strength.

Isaiah 46

2 Israelites could not deliver themselves, so they bowed down and went into captivity.

5 Whom will you liken to the Lord? Who could be like him?

9 Remember the former things of old, for I am God, and there is none else; I am God, and there is none like me.

10 I declare the end from the beginning and from ancient times the things that are not yet done, saying, My counsel shall stand, and I will do all I please.

11 The man who executes my counsel I will bring it to be; I have purposed it, and I will also do it.

12 Listen to me, you who are so strong, yet so far from righteousness.

Isaiah 48

12 Listen to me, Israel, I have called you; I am God. I am the first and last.
17 The LORD, your Redeemer, the Holy One of Israel, says, I am the
LORD your God who teaches you to profit, who leads you in the way that
you should go.

Isaiah 49

4 Then I said, I have labored in vain. I have spent my strength for nothing;
surely my judgment is with the LORD, and my work is with my God.
23 Know that I am the LORD, for those who wait for me shall not be
ashamed.

Isaiah 50

4 The Lord GOD has given me the voice of the educated, that I should
know how to speak compassionately to him who is weary.

Isaiah 52

7 How beautiful upon the mountains are the feet of him who brings good
news, who proclaims peace and salvation, saying to Zion, Your God reigns!
10 The LORD has exposed his holy arm in the eyes of all the nations, so
all the ends of the earth shall see the salvation of our God.
12 You shall not go out speedily, for the LORD will go before you, and the
God of Israel will be your reward.

Isaiah 53

6 Visualize this, we are all like sheep and have gone astray; we have turned everyone to his own way, and God has laid upon him (Christ) the iniquity of us all.
7 He (Christ) was oppressed and afflicted, yet he opened not his mouth; he
was brought as a lamb to the slaughter, and as a sheep before her shearers
was dumb, so he opened not his mouth.
8 He (Christ) was taken from prison and from judgment; he was cut off
from the land of the living to die for the sins of his people.
9 He (Christ) made his grave with the wicked and with the rich in his death;
because he had done no violence, neither was any deceit in his mouth.
11 He (Christ) shall see the deep yearnings of his soul and shall be satisfied; by his knowledge shall my righteous servant justify many, for he shall
bear their iniquities.

Isaiah 54

10 The mountains shall depart and the hills removed, but my kindness shall not leave you; neither shall the covenant of my peace be removed, says the LORD, who has mercy on you.

Isaiah 55

6 Seek the LORD while he may be found; call upon him while he is near.
7 Let the wicked forsake his ways and the unrighteous man his thoughts. Let him return to the LORD, and the LORD will have mercy upon him, for he will abundantly pardon.
8 My thoughts are not your thoughts; neither are my ways your ways, says the LORD.
9 As the heavens are higher than the earth, so are my ways higher than your ways and my thoughts higher than your thoughts.
11 So shall my Word be true that goes out of my mouth; it shall not return to me void, but it shall accomplish that which I please, and it shall prosper wherever I send it.

Isaiah 56

1 The LORD says, Keep your word and do justice, for my salvation is near, and my righteousness will be revealed.
2 Blessed is the man who does this and keeps his hand from doing evil.

Isaiah 57

1 The righteous man perishes, and no man cares. Merciful men are taken away, yet none consider the evil to come.

Isaiah 58

10 If you direct your soul to care for the hungry, then shall your light shine, and the darkness shall become bright as high noon.
11 The LORD shall guide you continually and satisfy your soul when it seems dry; you shall be like an ever flowing spring of water.
13 Keep the sabbath; put away your worldly pleasures on my holy day. Call the sabbath a delight, the honorable holy day of the LORD. You shall honor him by not going your own ways, finding your own pleasure, or speaking your own words.

Isaiah 59

1 Good news. The LORD's hand is not shortened, that it cannot save; neither is his ear heavy, that it cannot hear.

20 The Redeemer shall come to Zion and to those who turn from sin, says the LORD.

Isaiah 61

8 I, the LORD, love judgment. I will direct my people's work in truth, and I will make an everlasting covenant with them.

Isaiah 62

12 They shall call them the holy people, the redeemed of the LORD.

Isaiah 63

7 I will tell of the loving kindnesses of the LORD, according to all that he has given us.

Isaiah 64

4 Since the beginning of the world, men have not heard nor seen what God has prepared for those who seek him.

5 You will meet God; you who rejoice, work righteousness, and remember him in your ways, but God is angry because we continually sin. How shall we be saved?

9 Please do not be angry, LORD; neither remember our sins forever, for we are your people.

Isaiah 65

2 I continually spread out my hands to a rebellious people who walk in ways that are not good, after their own thoughts.

Isaiah 66

1-2 The LORD says, The sky is my throne, and the earth is my footstool. He also asks, Where is the house that you built for me that I may rest? These are those things that my hands have made. Must I look to the man who is poor and of a contrite spirit, who trembles at my Word?

3 Man's idea of sin offerings to God is not according to God's request. Man's soul delights in created offerings that are an abomination to the LORD.

15 Behold, the LORD will come with blazing fire and chariots to release his anger.

16 By fire and by sword will the LORD plead with all people, and those killed shall be many.

Jeremiah

Jeremiah was one of God's prophets. In Chapters 14 and 23, he exposes false prophets. Some of today's church leaders and their followers continually use a phrase similar to "God told me this or that," or "You are healed of this or that." Some are often speaking lies from their own invention. Today, we see false churches that have a leadership position labeled as Prophet. Jeremiah has warned us to discern who is a false prophet. He says not to follow any prophet who has given a false prophecy because that prophet is not God's prophet. There are millions of people today who allow themselves to follow false prophets because they do not test them by their words for truth.

Jeremiah 1

5 The Lord said, Jeremiah, before I formed you in the womb, I knew you. Before you came forth out of the womb, I sanctified you, and I ordained you a prophet to the nations.

Jeremiah 3

23 Truly in the LORD our God is the salvation of Israel.

Jeremiah 5

23-24 Let us fear the LORD our God, who gives rain, both the former and the latter in his season; he reserves to us the appointed weeks of the harvest.

Jeremiah 10

6 There is none, no not one, like the LORD; he is great, and his name is mighty.

10 The LORD is the true God; he is the living God and an everlasting king; at his anger the earth shall tremble.

11 Say to them, The gods that have not made the heavens and the earth shall perish.

12 God has made the earth by his power and established it by his wisdom. He has stretched out the heavens according to his plan.
24 LORD, correct me with judgment, but not in your anger; that would bring me to nothing.

Jeremiah 13

11 As tight pants fit close to a man's leg, so have I caused Israel to be close to me, says the LORD; that they might be to me a people, a name, a praise, and a glory, but they would not listen.
16 Give glory to the LORD your God before he causes your darkness to become absolute black darkness.

Jeremiah 14

14 Then the LORD said to me, The prophets foretell lies in my name; I did not send them; neither have I commanded them. They prophesy to you false visions and divinations out of the deceit of their heart.
15 The LORD says, I sent them not, yet they say, Sword and famine shall not be in this land; by sword and famine shall those prophets be consumed.
22 Are there any creations of man that can cause significant rains? Is he not the LORD our God? So wait upon him, for he made all things.

Jeremiah 15

19 The LORD says, If you return to me, I will strengthen you. If you take my Word to be my representative, let the people come to you.

Jeremiah 16

19 LORD, you are my strength, fortress, and refuge in the day of trouble. The Gentiles shall come to you from everywhere saying, Our fathers have inherited lies that do not profit us.

Jeremiah 17

5 The LORD says, Cursed is the man who does not trust the LORD and makes flesh his strength. His heart has rejected the LORD.
7 Blessed is he who trusts and hopes in the LORD.
9-10 The heart is deceitful above all things and desperately wicked; who can know it? The LORD searches the heart and pulls it to him. He gives to every man according to his ways and according to the results of his actions.

14 Heal me, oh LORD, and I shall be healed; save me, and I shall be saved, for you are my praise.

22 Do not carry your burdens out of your home on the sabbath day; neither do any work, but make the sabbath day holy as I commanded your fathers.

Jeremiah 23

23 I am a personal God, says the LORD; I am not a God who is far off.

24 Can any man hide himself in secret so I can not see him, says the LORD? Know that I fill heaven and earth.

25-27 I have heard what the prophets said. They prophesy lies in God's name, saying, I have dreamed; I have dreamed. How long shall this be? These are false prophets of deceit. They devise to cause my people to forget my name by their dreams, which they tell every man to his neighbor.

28 The prophet who has a dream, let him tell his dream; He who has my Word, let him speak my Word faithfully, says the LORD.

30-32 Pay attention, I am against these prophets who steal my words. I am against the prophets who use their tongues to say that God is saying this. Behold, I, the LORD, am against those who prophesy false dreams. They cause my people to error by their lies. I sent them not, nor commanded them to speak for me; know that they shall not profit the people at all, says the LORD.

Jeremiah 27

9-10 Do not listen to prophets, diviners, dreamers, enchanters, or sorcerers. These people prophesy lies to you. They will cause you to perish.

Jeremiah 28

9 By his prophesies, know that when the words of that prophet come true, the LORD truly had sent him.

Jeremiah 29

11 I know the thoughts that I have toward you, says the LORD, thoughts of peace and not of evil, to give you an expected end.

Jeremiah 31

13 Then shall the virgin rejoice in the dance, both young men and old

together. I will turn sadness into joy, and the LORD will comfort them and make them rejoice out of their sorrow.

30 Everyone shall die for his own sins; every man who eats the sour grape, his teeth shall be set on edge.

Jeremiah 32

38 Israelites shall be my people, and I will be their God.

39 I will give them one heart and one way, that they may fear me forever, for the good of them and for their children after them.

Jeremiah 33

10-11 The LORD says about Judah and Jerusalem, There will be heard once more the voice of joy of the bride, her groom, and those who shall say, Praise the LORD of hosts. The LORD is good. His mercy endures forever. To those who bring the sacrifice of praise into the house of the LORD, I will cause the return of the captivity of the land, as it was at the first when I established them.

Jeremiah 42

6 Whether it be pleasing or displeasing us, we will obey the voice of the LORD, our God, that it may be well with us when we obey.

Jeremiah 46

28 Fear not, Jacob my servant, says the LORD, for I am with you. I will make a full end of all the nations from where I have driven you. I will not make a full end of you but correct you in my time. But I will not leave you altogether unpunished.

Jeremiah 51

15 God has made the earth by his power; he has established the world by his wisdom and has stretched out space by his understanding.

16 When God knows there is a multitude of water, he causes vapor to ascend up from of the earth; then he makes lightnings and rain and brings forth the wind out of his treasures.

56 Because the enemy comes, the God of justice shall surely take revenge.

Lamentations

Lamentations has great verses for in-depth thought. This book helps us understand Christ as our advocate before a holy God.

Lamentations 2

22 In the day of the LORD's anger, none shall escape nor remain; those who were my enemy will be consumed.

Lamentations 3

22 It is due to the LORD's mercies that we are not consumed because his compassion does not fail.
23 His mercies are new every morning; great is his faithfulness.
24 The LORD is my provider, says my soul; therefore, will I hope in him.
25 The LORD is good to those who wait for him, to the soul who seeks him.
26 It is good that a man should both hope in and quietly wait for the salvation of the LORD.
27 It is good for a man to be accountable for his bad deeds when he is young.
31 The LORD will not abandon you forever.
32 Even though the LORD causes you grief, he will have compassion according to the greatness of his mercies.
40 Let us think about our ways, test them, and turn again to the LORD.
41-42 Let us lift up our heart with our hands to God in the heavens. We have sinned and rebelled, and you have not yet pardoned.
56 You have heard my voice, so do not hide your ear, but hear my cry.
57 You draw near in the day that I called upon you; you said to fear not.
58 LORD, you have pleaded the causes of my soul; you have redeemed my life.
59 LORD, you have seen my wrong ways; judge my cause.

Lamentations 5

19 LORD, you remain forever; your throne is from generation to generation.
21 LORD, turn us to you, and we shall be restored; renew the joy we knew.

Ezekiel

Ezekiel rejects the idea that man can become a god.

Ezekiel 28

2, 6, 9 The Lord says, Your heart is too proud, and you have said, I am a God; I sit in the seat of God, yet you are only a man and not God, This causes the Lord to say, Because you have set your heart as the heart of God, will you yet say before me that I am God? But you shall be a man, and not a god in my hand which will slay you.

11 The Lord says, Behold, I, even I, will both search my sheep and seek them out. As a shepherd seeks out his scattered flock in the day that he is among them, so will I seek out my sheep and will deliver them out of all places where they have been scattered.

26 I will make them a blessing and will cause the rain to come down in its season; there shall be showers of blessing.

Ezekiel 36

26-27 I will give you a new heart and put a new spirit in you; I will re-move from you your heart of stone and give you a heart of flesh. I will put my Spirit in you and move you to follow my decrees.

Daniel

Our God is an awesome God.

Daniel 2

20 Daniel answered and said, Blessed be the name of God forever and ever, for wisdom and might are his.

21 He changes the times and the seasons; he removes kings and sets up kings; he gives wisdom to the wise and knowledge to those who know understanding.

Daniel 4

34 At the end of the days I, Nebuchadnezzar, lifted up my eyes to heaven, and my understanding returned to me. I blessed the Most High God, and I praised and honored him who lives forever, whose rule is an everlasting rule, and whose kingdom is from generation to generation.

Daniel 6

26 I make a statement that in every corner of my kingdom men shake with fear before the God of Daniel; his God is the living God who is steadfast forever; his kingdom shall not be destroyed, and his rule shall never end.
27 God delivers and rescues, and he works signs and wonders in heaven and on earth. He has delivered Daniel from the power of the lions.

Daniel 7

9 I saw the Ancient of Days sitting. God's garment was white as snow; the hair of his head was like pure wool; his throne was like a blazing fire, and his wheels were as burning fire.

Daniel 9

4 I prayed to the LORD and made my confession; he is the great and dreadful God, keeping his covenant and giving his mercy to those who love him and keep his commandments.
7 LORD, righteousness belongs to you, but we do not understand it. The men of Judah, Jerusalem, and all Israel are where you have driven them because they have trespassed against you.

Daniel 12

2 Many who are dead shall awake, some to everlasting life and some to shame and everlasting rejection.
3 Those who are wise shall shine bright like the sun at noon, and those who turn many to righteousness shall shine like stars forever and ever.

Hosea

Again, God tells us that he wants an intimate relationship with us.

Hosea 2

19 I will marry you forever; yes, I will marry you to me in righteousness, in judgment, in loving kindness, and in mercies.
20 I will marry you, due to your faith, and you shall know the LORD.

Hosea 11

9 I will not execute the fierceness of my anger; I will not return to destroy
Ephraim, for I am God and not man. I am the Holy One in the midst of you.
10 They shall live following the LORD; the LORD shall roar like a lion,
and the people shall respond with fear.

Hosea 12

6 Turn to God; keep mercy and judgment, and continually follow God's
leading.

Hosea 13

4 I am the LORD your God from the land of Egypt, and you shall know no
god but me, for there is no savior beside me.

Hosea 14

1 Oh Israel, return to the LORD your God, for you have fallen by your
iniquity.
3 We will not say any more about the works of our hand. You are our gods,
for in God the fatherless finds mercy.
9 Who is wise and prudent to understand these things? The ways of the
LORD are right, and the just shall walk in them, but the sinners shall fall.

Joel

Joel prophecies the second coming of Jesus Christ, even before Christ
comes the first time. We are warned to be ready for that event.

Joel 1

15 The Day of the LORD is at hand, and this day of destruction shall come
from the Almighty.

Joel 2

11 The LORD shall give his command to his great army, for he is strong
and executes his Word. The day of the LORD is great and very terrible, and
who can survive?

12 Now, says the LORD, Turn to me with your whole heart and with fasting, weeping, and mourning.

13 Give your heart, not your clothes, and turn to the LORD your God. He is gracious and merciful, slow to get angry, and displays great kindness.

21 Fear not; be glad and rejoice, for the LORD will do great things.

27 You shall know that I am in the middle of Israel. I am the LORD your God, and none else. My people shall never be ashamed.

28 It shall come, when I will pour out my spirit upon all flesh, and your sons and daughters shall prophesy. Your old men shall dream dreams, and your young men shall see visions.

Joel 3

10 Beat your steel plows into swords and your tree pruners into spears; let the weak say, I am strong.

Amos

Amos confirms that God is mighty and to be feared.

Amos 5

14 Seek good and not evil, so that you may live, and the LORD, the God of his armies, shall be with you as you have spoken.

15 Hate evil, love good, and establish judgment in the city.

Obadiah

Obadiah warns the world of the results of wrong choices when Christ comes again. God's judgment and wrath will not be avoidable.

Obadiah 1

15 The Day of the LORD is near upon all the heathen; as you have done, it shall be done to you; your reward shall return upon your own head.

Jonah

Jonah respected and trusted God.

Jonah 2

1 Then Jonah prayed to the LORD his God when he was in the fish's belly.
9 I will sacrifice to you with the voice of thanksgiving; I will pay that
which I have vowed. Salvation is of the LORD.

Micah

Micah affirms that God is a God of justice.

Micah 1

3 Behold, the LORD comes out of his place. He will come down and stand
firm upon the high places of the earth.

Micah 4

3 God shall judge many people and reject strong nations, and they shall
beat their swords into plowshares and their spears into pruning tools. A nation
shall not lift up a sword against another nation; neither shall they learn war
any more.

Micah 6

8 God has shown you what is good, so what does the LORD require of
you? Do justly, love mercy, and walk humbly with your God.

Micah 7

7 Therefore, I will look to the LORD; I will wait for the God of my salvation
and my God will hear me.

Nahum

The prophet Nahum warns us that God will rule against sin.

Nahum 1

2 God is jealous; he takes revenge on his enemies because he is furious.
3 But the LORD is slow to anger and great in power. He will not find the

wicked guiltless. The LORD controls the whirlwind and the storm, and the clouds are the dust of his feet.

6 Who can stand before God's anger? Who can exist in the fierceness of his anger? His fury is poured out like fire, and the rocks are thrown down by him.

7 The LORD is good; he is a strong fort in the day of trouble, and he knows those who trust in him.

Habakkuk

The prophet Habakkuk waited upon God to serve justice upon his enemies. He displayed great faith and respect for God. In chapter 3 he describes the Lord's power.

Habakkuk 2

2 The LORD answered me and said, Write the vision, and make it plainly written, that he who reads it may run.

3 The vision is yet for an appointed time, but at the end it shall speak and not lie; though it comes slowly, wait for it because it will surely come.

4 Notice, his soul is puffed up and not trustworthy, but the just man shall live by faith.

20 The LORD is in his holy temple; let all the earth keep silence before him.

Habakkuk 3

3-6 God came from Teman and the Holy One from Mount Paran. His glory covered the heavens, and the earth was full of his praise. His brightness was as the light; he had horns coming out of his hand, and in them was the hiding of his power. Before him went pest infestation, and burning coals spread out in front of his feet. He stood and measured the earth; he drove out the nations, and the everlasting mountains were scattered; the perpetual hills did fall down; his ways are everlasting.

18-19 I will rejoice in the LORD, the God of my salvation. The LORD is my strength, and he will make me able to walk upon higher ground.

Zephaniah

Zephaniah lived in the shadow of Almighty God. He enjoyed his personal relationship with God and encourages us to do the same.

Zephaniah 2

3 Seek the LORD, all you who are the meek of the earth. You have brought God's judgment, so seek righteousness and meekness, that you may escape the Day of the LORD's anger.

Zephaniah 3

5 The LORD is just; he cannot sin. Every morning he brings his judgment to light; and yet, the unjust knows no shame.

17 The LORD your God is mighty; he will save. He will rejoice over you with joy. He will rest you in his love, and He will rejoice over you with singing.

Haggai

Haggai is a small but wonderful book. It tells us that man's ways without God amount to nothing, but when we trust in God, he is our strength and refuge. God wants a personal relationship with us, and will overthrow our enemies.

Haggai 1

1-4 The word of the LORD came by Haggai saying, These people say, The time has not come to build the LORD's house. Then came the word of the LORD by Haggai the prophet, saying, Is it first time for you to dwell in your own houses, while the LORD'S house lies in ruins?

5-6 This says the LORD of hosts, Consider your ways: You have sown much and bring in little; you eat, but you do not have enough. You drink, but you are not filled; you put on clothes, but you are not warm. What sense would it be to earn wages and put them in a bag that has holes in it?

Haggai 2

4-5 Work, for I am with you, says the LORD of hosts. My spirit remains among you, so fear not.

6-8 In a little while I will shake the heavens and the earth. I will shake all nations, and I will fill this earth with glory, says the LORD of hosts. The silver is mine, and the gold is mine.

21-22 I will shake the heavens and the earth. I will overthrow the throne of kingdoms, and I will destroy the strength of the kingdoms of the heathen.

Zechariah

Zechariah was a great prophet. His book is filled with detailed prophesies about Christ. Read it all and see that Christ fulfilled these prophesies some 400 years before the NEW TESTAMENT events.

Zechariah 4

6 Then God answered me, saying, This is the Word of the LORD: Not by might, nor by power, but by my spirit, says the LORD of hosts.

Zechariah 9

9 Rejoice greatly, oh daughters of Zion; shout, oh daughters of Jerusalem; behold, your King comes to you. He is just and has salvation; he is lowly and comes riding upon a donkey.

Zechariah 11

11-12 It was broken in that day, and so the poor of the flock who waited upon me knew that it was the Word of the LORD. And I said to them, If you think it is good, give me my price, and if not, be patient. So they weighed for my price thirty pieces of silver.

Malachi

Malachi is the final book of the prophets in the OLD TESTAMENT. Following it are some 400 silent years of biblical history before Christ comes to die on the cross, offering redemption for man's sins. These long silent years establish the authenticity of all the prophesies about Christ.

Malachi 2

10 Have we not all one father? Has not one God created us? Why do we deal treacherously against our brother, by profaning the covenant of our fathers? 16 The LORD, the God of Israel, says that he hates divorce, for one covers anger and violence with his garment. Take heed to your spirit that you do not betray and deceive.

HIGHLIGHTING THE GOOD NEWS

(KJV)
Abbreviated, Paraphrased, and Edited

NEW TESTAMENT

Within the NEW TESTAMENT, the "us" and "our" in Genesis is answered. They are the triune nature of God -- God the Father, God the Son, and God the Holy Spirit. God's Word can be trusted. Truth is an attribute of God. He will not violate his Word.

The OLD TESTAMENT contains the Laws of God, which leave no person sinless. But, God's grace is then understood in its fullness in the NEW TESTAMENT. Here, faith in Christ's atonement for our sin makes us right before God.

The NEW TESTAMENT is about our opportunity to have a personal relationship with God, who is absolute in every one of his attributes. It is understanding absolute love, truth and holiness that explain why Christ has to be God.

No other religion in the world can give man the total answers to life and existence. Those answers are all in the *Holy Bible*.

The books of Matthew, Mark, Luke and John tell the story of Jesus Christ from his birth to just shortly after his death. Each writer gives his own perspective as inspired by God. Read and hear Christ speak to you.

Matthew

Matthew 1

23 Behold, a virgin shall give birth to a son, and they shall call his name Emmanuel, which means God with us.

Matthew 2

1 When Jesus was born in Bethlehem, there came wise men from the east to honor him.

Matthew 3

2 When John the Baptist saw Jesus Christ, he said to his listeners, Repent, for the kingdom of heaven is near.

3 This is the Christ who was spoken of by the prophet, Isaiah, saying, Prepare the way of the Lord.

10 Every tree that does not produce good fruit is cut down and cast into the fire.

11 I, John, baptize the people with water for repentance, but he who comes after me is mightier than I, whose shoes I am not worthy to wear; he shall baptize you with the Holy Ghost and with fire.

16 Jesus, when he was baptized, came up out of the water. The skies opened, and the people saw the Spirit of God descending like a dove and resting upon him.

17 Then a voice came from heaven, saying, This is my Son, whom I love, with whom I am well pleased.

Matthew 4

4 Jesus spent 40 days in the wilderness. While there, the Devil came to tempt him, so Jesus said to him, It is written: Man shall not live by bread alone but by every word that proceeds out of the mouth of God.

7 Jesus said to the Devil, It is written again: You shall not tempt the Lord your God.

Matthew 5

3 Jesus taught the crowd, Blessed are the poor in spirit, for theirs is the kingdom of heaven.

4 Blessed are those who mourn, for they shall be comforted.

5 Blessed are the meek, for they shall inherit the earth.

6 Blessed are those who do hunger and thirst after righteousness, for they shall be filled.

7 Blessed are the merciful, for they shall obtain mercy.

8 Blessed are the pure in heart, for they shall see God.

9 Blessed are the peacemakers, for they shall be called the children of God.

10 Blessed are those who are persecuted for righteousness' sake, for theirs is the kingdom of heaven.

11 Blessed are you when men shall insult you, persecute you, and say all manner of evil against you falsely, but it is for my purpose.

12 Rejoice and be exceeding glad, for great is your reward in heaven; they persecuted the prophets who were before you.

13 You are the salt of the earth, but if the salt has lost its taste, how shall it

regain it? After that it is good for nothing, so throw it out.

14 You are the light of the world. A city that is set on a hill cannot be hid.

16 Let your light so shine before men that they may see your good works and glorify your Father who is in heaven.

17 Think not that I came to destroy the law or the prophets; I did not come to destroy, but to fulfill it.

18 Truly I say to you, Until heaven and earth pass away, not one thing shall be removed from the law until all of it is fulfilled.

21-22 You have heard it said years ago, You shall not kill, and whoever shall kill shall be in danger of the judgment. But I say to you, Whoever is angry with his brother without a cause shall be in danger of the judgment, and whoever shall say to his brother, Raca, shall be in danger of the council, but whoever shall say, You fool, shall be in danger of hell fire.

23-24 If you bring your gift to the altar and there remember that your brother has something against you, leave your gift before the altar and go your way; first be reconciled to your brother, and then come again and offer your gift.

25 Agree with your critic quickly while you are with him, unless at any time the critic deliver you to the judge and the judge deliver you to the officer to put you in prison.

28 I say to you, Whoever looks upon a woman to lust after her has committed adultery with her already in his heart.

29 If your right eye offends you, take it out and throw it away, for it is more profitable that one of your body parts should perish than your whole body be thrown into hell.

30 If your right hand offends you, cut it off and throw it away, for it is more profitable that one of your members should perish than your whole body should be thrown into hell.

32 I say to you, Whoever shall put away his wife, except for the cause of fornication, causes her to commit adultery, and whoever shall marry her who is divorced commits adultery.

33 Again, you have heard that it has been said by them years ago, You shall not swear by yourself, but shall perform to the Lord your oaths.

37 Let your communication be yes or no, for whatever is more than these comes from the Devil.

39 I say to you, Do not resist evil, but he who strikes you on your right cheek, turn to him the other also.

40 If any man will sue you with the law and take away your coat, let him have your sweater also.

41 Whoever shall force you to go a mile, go with him two.

42 Give to him who asks you, and from him who would borrow from you, turn him not away.

44 I say to you, Love your enemies; bless those who curse you. Do good to those who hate you. Pray for those who despitefully use you and persecute you.
46 If you love those who love you, what reward have you? Do not the publicans do the same?
47 If you salute your friends only, how are you better than others?
48 Be perfect, even as God our Father, who is in heaven, is perfect.

Matthew 6

1 Do not give your offerings so others can see the amount; otherwise, you have no reward from your Father who is in heaven.
2 When you do your giving, do not sound a trumpet as the hypocrites do that they may have the glory of men. I say to you, They have their reward.
3 When you give, do not let your left hand know what your right hand does.
6 When you pray, enter into your closet, and when you have shut the door, pray to your Father who is in secret. Your Father, who sees in secret, shall reward you openly.
14 If you forgive men their sins, your heavenly Father will also forgive you.
19 Do not lay up for yourselves treasures upon earth, where moth and rust destroy it and where thieves break through and steal it.
21 Where your treasure is, there your heart is also.
22 The light of the body is the eye; if your eye is controlled, your whole body shall be full of light.
24 No man can serve two masters, for either he will hate the one and love the other, or he will hold to the one and despise the other. You cannot serve God and money.
25, 27 I say to you, Take no thought for your life, what you shall eat or what you shall drink; nor for your body, what you shall put on. Is not life more than just eating meat and the body more than your clothes? Which of you by taking thought can add one measure to his body's height?
30 If God clothes the grass of the field, which today exists and tomorrow is thrown into the fire, shall he not much more clothe you? Oh you of little faith.
33 Seek first the kingdom of God and his righteousness, and all these things shall be given to you.
34 Take no thought for tomorrow, for tomorrow shall take care of itself. Sufficient for this day is the evil of it.

Matthew 7

1 Judge not, that you be not judged.
3 Why do you see the speck that is in your brother's eye, but consider not the beam that is in your own eye?

6 Do not give that which is holy to the dogs; neither throw your pearls before swine, for they will trample them under their feet and turn again and run at you.

7 Ask, and it shall be given you; seek, and you shall find; knock, and it shall be opened to you.

9 What man is there among you, whom if his son asks for bread will he give him a stone?

12 All things whatsoever you ask that men should do to you, you do the same to them, for this is the law and the prophet's teaching.

13-14 Enter in at the strait gate, for wide is the gate and broad is the way which lead to destruction, and many enter there. Strait is the gate and narrow is the way which lead to life, and few there be who find it.

15-16 Beware of false prophets who come to you in sheep's clothing, but inwardly they are vicious wolves. You shall know them by their fruits.

19 Every tree that does not produce good fruit is cut down and thrown into the fire.

21 Not everyone who says to me, Lord, Lord, shall enter into the kingdom of heaven, but he who does the will of my Father who is in heaven shall enter.

22-23 Many will say to me in that day, Lord, Lord, have we not prophesied, cast out devils, and done many wonderful works in your name? And then will I tell them, I never knew you. Depart from me, you who work iniquity.

24 Whoever hears these sayings of mine and does them, I will liken him to a wise man who built his house upon a rock.

26 Everyone who hears these sayings of mine and does not do them, shall be likened to a foolish man who built his house upon the sand.

Matthew 8

22 Jesus said to him, Follow me, and let the dead bury their dead.

Matthew 9

13 Jesus said, I will have mercy and not sacrifice, for I did not come to call the righteous, but sinners to repentance.

37 Then said Jesus to his disciples, The harvest truly is plentiful, but the laborers are few.

38 Pray that the Lord of the harvest will send out laborers into his harvest.

Matthew 10

8 Heal the sick, cleanse the lepers, raise the dead, and cast out devils; freely you have received, freely give.

22 You shall be hated by all men for my name's sake, but he who endures to the end shall be saved.

24-25 The disciple is not above his master, nor the servant above his lord. It is enough for the disciple that he be like his master and the servant like his lord.

26 Fear not, for there is nothing covered that shall not be revealed and nothing hid that shall not be made known.

28 Fear not those who kill the body but are not able to kill the soul. Fear him who is able to destroy both the body and the soul in hell.

32 Whoever shall confess me before men, him will I confess before my Father who is in heaven.

34 Do not think that I have come to bring peace on earth; I came not to bring peace, but a sword.

35-38 I have come to set a son against his father, a daughter against her mother, and a daughter-in-law against her mother-in-law. A man's foes shall be of his own household. He who loves father or mother more than me is not worthy of me, and he who loves son or daughter more than me is not worthy of me. He who does not take up his cross and follow after me is not worthy of me.

39 He who finds his life shall lose it, and he who loses his life for my purpose shall find it.

42 Whoever shall give one small cup of cold water to one of these little ones in the name of a disciple shall in no way lose his reward.

Matthew 11

11 Surely I say to you, Among those who are born of women there has not come a greater one than John the Baptist, but know this: He who is least in the kingdom of heaven is greater than John.

27 All things are delivered to me from my Father. No man knows the Son but the Father. Neither does any man know the Father except the Son and those to whom the Son will reveal the Father.

28-30 Come to me all you who labor and are heavy laden, and I will give you rest. Take my yoke upon you and learn of me, for I am meek and lowly in heart, and in me you shall find rest for your souls. My yoke is easy, and my burden is light.

Matthew 12

25 Jesus knew their thoughts and said to them, Every kingdom divided against itself is brought to desolation, and every city or house divided against itself shall not stand.

30 He who is not with me is against me, and he who does not gather with me scatters afar.

31 I say to you, All manner of sin and blasphemy shall be forgiven men, but the blasphemy against the Holy Ghost shall not be forgiven men.

32 Whoever speaks a word against the Son of Man, it shall be forgiven him, but whoever speaks against the Holy Ghost, it shall not be forgiven him; neither in this world, nor in the world to come.

(Definition: The Son of Man is Christ because he was conceived by God's Holy Spirit and born only through the virgin Mary. He is also spoken of as the Son of God because he is God manifesting himself in the flesh as Christ and born for God's perfect plan of salvation to redeem man from his sins)

33 Christ said, Make the tree good and its fruit good or else make the tree corrupt and its fruit corrupt, for the tree is known by its fruit.

35 A good man out of the good treasure of his heart brings forth good things, and an evil man out of the evil treasure brings forth evil things.

36-37 I say to you, Every idle word that men speak, they shall give account for in the day of judgment. It is by your words that you shall be justified, and it is by your words that you shall be condemned.

Matthew 13

16 Blessed are your eyes, for they see and your ears, for they hear.

57 The people were offended by him, but Jesus said to them, A prophet is not without honor, except in his own country and in his own house.

Matthew 15

4 God commanded saying, Honor your father and mother. He who curses father or mother let him die the death.

18-19 Those things which proceed out of the mouth come from the heart, and they defile the man. Out of the heart proceed evil thoughts, murders, adulteries, fornications, thefts, false witnesses, and blasphemies.

26 Jesus answered and said, It is not right to take the children's bread and throw it to the dogs.

Matthew 16

19 I will give you the keys of the kingdom of heaven, and whatever you shall bind on earth shall be bound in heaven. Whatever you shall loose on earth shall be loosed in heaven.

27 The Son of Man shall come in the glory of his Father, with his angels, and shall reward every man according to his works.

Matthew 17

5 While he was still speaking, a bright cloud overshadowed them, and a voice out of the cloud said, This is my beloved Son, in whom I am well pleased. Hear him.

20 Jesus said to them, Because of your unbelief, if you have faith like a grain of mustard seed, you shall say to this mountain, Remove now to that place, and it shall move. Nothing shall be impossible to you.

Matthew 18

3 Surely I say to you, Except you are converted and become as little children, you shall not enter into the kingdom of heaven.

7 Woe to the world because of offenses, for offenses will come, but woe to that man by whom the offense comes!

8 If your hand or your foot offend you, cut it off and throw it away; it is better for you to enter into life handicapped, than to have two hands or two feet and be thrown into everlasting fire.

9 If your eye offends you, pull it out and throw it away. It is better for you to enter into life with one eye, than to have two eyes and be thrown into hell fire.

15-16 If your brother sins against you, go and tell him his fault between you and him alone. If he shall hear you, you have gained your brother, but if he will not hear you, then take with you one or two more so that by the mouth of two or three witnesses every word may be established.

19 Again I say to you, If two of you shall agree on earth concerning anything that people shall ask of you, it shall be done for them by my Father who is in heaven.

20 Where two or three are gathered together in my name, there am I in the middle of them.

21-22 Then came Peter and said, Lord, how often shall my brother sin against me and I forgive him? Until seven times? Jesus said to him, Not until seventy times seven.

Matthew 19

9 I say to you, Whoever shall put away his wife, except for forrnication, and shall marry another, commits adultery. Whoever marries her who is put away commits adultery.

14 Jesus said, Allow the little children and forbid them not to come to me, for of such is the kingdom of heaven.

17 Jesus said to the man, Why call me good? There is none good but one, and that is God. But you who enter into life are to keep the commandments.

21 Jesus said to him, If you will be perfect, go and sell what you have and give to the poor. Then you shall have treasure in heaven. Come and follow me.
23 Then said Jesus to his disciples, Surely I say to you, a rich man shall barely enter into the kingdom of heaven.
26 Jesus saw them and said, With men this is impossible, but with God all things are possible.
29 Everyone who has given up houses, brothers, sisters, father, mother, wife, children, or lands for my purposes shall receive a hundred times and shall inherit everlasting life.

Matthew 20

16 The last shall be first, and the first shall be last. Many are called, but few are chosen.
26-27 Whoever will be great among you, let him be your minister, and whoever will be chief among you, let him be your servant.
28 The Son of Man, (Christ), came not to be ministered to but to minister and to give his life a ransom for many.

Matthew 21

21 Jesus answered and said to them, I say to you, if you have faith and doubt not, you shall say to this mountain, Be removed and thrown into the sea, and it shall be done.
22 All things, whatsoever you shall ask in prayer, believing, you shall receive.
42 Jesus said to them, Did you not read in the scriptures, The stone which the builders rejected is the same that has become the corner stone? This is the Lord's doing and is marvellous in our eyes.
43 I say to you, The kingdom of God shall be taken from you and given to a nation bringing forth the fruits the kingdom.

Matthew 22

21 They asked Jesus about paying taxes to the government. He answered, Give to Caesar the things which are Caesar's and to God the things that are God's.
30 About marriage in heaven, Jesus said, In the resurrection they neither marry nor are given in marriage, but they are as the angels of God in heaven.
36-37, 39 Master, which is the great commandment in the law? Jesus said to the man, You shall love the Lord your God with all your heart, with all your soul, and with all your mind. And the second is like it; you shall love your neighbor as yourself.

Matthew 24

5 Many shall come in my name saying, I am Christ. They shall deceive many.

11 Many false prophets shall rise up and deceive many.

12 Because sin shall be everywhere, the love of many shall grow cold.

13-14 He who endures to the end, the same shall be saved. And this gospel of the kingdom shall be preached in all the world for a witness to all nations, and then shall the end come.

23-25 If any man shall say to you, here is Christ, or there he is, believe it not, for there shall arise false Christs and false prophets. They shall show great signs and wonders, so much so that if it were possible, they shall deceive the very elect. Notice, I have told you this before it happens.

37 As the days of Noah were, so shall the coming of the Son of Man be.

42 I say, Watch, for you know not what hour your Lord comes.

44 Be ready, for in the hour you think not, the Son of Man comes.

Matthew 25

21 His lord said to him, Well done, good and faithful servant. You have been faithful over a few things; I will make you ruler over many things. Enter into the joy of your lord.

31 When the Son of Man shall come in his glory and all the holy angels with him, then shall he sit upon the throne of his glory.

46 Unbelievers shall go away into everlasting punishment, but the righteous believers into life eternal.

Matthew 26

11 You have the poor always with you, but me, you have not always.

24 The Son of Man goes as it is written of him, but fear will come to that man by whom the Son of Man is betrayed! It would have been better for that man if he had not been born.

Matthew 28

This chapter is written about events after Christ was crucified on the cross for man's sin. Prophesy in the OLD TESTAMENT foretold that this event would happen as it did. Without the cross, we would have no hope of any relationship with God.

19-20 Go and teach all nations, baptizing them in the name of the Father, and of the Son, and of the Holy Ghost. Teach them to observe all that I have commanded you, and, lo, I am with you always, even to the end of the world. Amen.

Mark

Find a quiet place to read the book of Mark. Contemplate Mark's writings, and listen anew for what Christ wants you to hear.

Mark 1

3 John is the voice of one crying in the wilderness, saying, Prepare the way of the Lord; make his paths straight.
15 And saying, The time is fulfilled, and the kingdom of God is at hand; repent and believe the gospel.

Mark 2

7 Why does this man Jesus speak blasphemies? Only God can forgive sins.
27-28 And Jesus said to them, The sabbath was made for man and not man for the sabbath. Therefore, the Son of Man is Lord of the sabbath, also.

Mark 3

35 Jesus said, Whoever shall do the will of God, the same is my brother, and my sister, and my mother.

Mark 7

6-8 Christ answered and said to the religious leaders, Esaias has prophesied well of you hypocrites, as it is written, These people honor me with their lips, but their heart is far from me. It is in vain that they worship me; they teach doctrines that are the commandments of men. You put aside the commandments of God, and you hold onto the traditions of men.
9 He said to them, You reject the commandments of God, so that you may keep your own traditions.
15 There is nothing outside of man that can defile him. It is the things which come out of him; those are what defile the man.

Mark 8

29 Jesus said to his disciples, But whom do you say who I am? And Peter
answered him, You are the Christ. (He is the promised Savior of the world
prophesied in the OLD TESTAMENT to come to earth. The Savior would save
man from just punishment relating to sin.)
34 When Jesus had called the people to himself he said, Whoever will
come after me, let him deny himself, take up his cross, and follow me.
35 Whoever will save his life shall lose it, but whoever shall lose his life
for my purposes and the gospel's, the same shall save his life.
36 What shall it profit a man if he gains the whole world and loses his own
soul?
37-38 What shall a man give in exchange for his soul? Whoever shall be
ashamed of me and of my words in this adulterous and sinful generation,
of him shall the Son of Man be ashamed when he comes in the glory of his
Father with the holy angels.

Mark 9

35 Jesus sat down, called his twelve disciples, and said to them, If any man
desires to be first, the same shall be last of all and the servant of all.
42 Whoever shall offend one of these little children who believes in me,
it would be better for him that a rock be hung around his neck, and him
thrown into the sea.
43 If your hand offends you, cut it off. It is better for you to enter into life
maimed, than having two hands to go into hell, which has fire that shall
never be quenched.
45 If your foot offends you, cut it off. It is better for you to live life
without it than to have two feet and be thrown into hell, which has fire that
shall never be quenched.
47 If your eye offends you, pull it out. It is better for you to enter into the
kingdom of God with one eye, than to have two eyes, and be thrown into
hell fire.
50 Salt is good, but if the salt has lost its saltness, where will you season it
again? Have salt in yourselves, and have peace one with another.

Mark 10

2-4 The religious Pharisees tempted Jesus saying, Is it lawful for a man
to put away his wife? He answered them, What did Moses command you?
They responded, Moses struggled to write a bill of divorcement.
5-8 Jesus said to them, Because of the hardness of your heart he wrote you

this precept, but from the beginning of the creation God made them male and female. For marriage a man shall leave his father and mother and hold fast to his wife, and they shall become one flesh. Now they are no more two separate individuals, but they are one flesh.

9, 11 Therefore, what God has joined together, let not man break that bond. Whoever shall put away his wife or husband and marry another commits adultery.

14-16 Jesus said to them, Allow the little children to come to me, and forbid them not, for of such is the kingdom of God. Surely I say to you, Whoever shall not receive the kingdom of God as a little child, he shall not enter it. And Jesus took the children up in his arms, put his hands upon them and blessed them.

18 Jesus said to a rich man when they met, Why do you call me good? There is none good but one; that is God.

21 Then Jesus gazed at this rich man and loved him, saying to him, One thing you lack; go your way, sell whatever you have, and give to the poor. Then you shall have treasure in heaven, and come, take up the cross and follow me.

25 Jesus said to his disciples, It is easier for a camel to go through the eye of a needle than for a rich man to enter into the kingdom of God.

27 Jesus looked upon the disciples saying, With men it is impossible, but with God all things are possible.

31 Many who are first shall be last and the last first.

40 To sit on my right hand and on my left hand is not mine to give, but it shall be given to them for whom it is prepared.

43 Whoever will be great among you shall be your minister.

45 Even the Son of Man came not to be ministered to, but to minister and to give his life a ransom for many.

Mark 11

9 Those who went in front, and those who followed Jesus shouted, Hosanna. Blessed is he who comes in the name of the Lord.

24 I say to you, Whatever things you desire, when you pray, believe that you receive them, and you shall have them.

25 When you stand praying, forgive those who have sinned against you, so that your Father who is in heaven may forgive you your sins.

Mark 12

10-11 Jesus said, Have you not read this scripture: The stone which the builders rejected has become the head of the corner?

17 Jesus answered his questioners, Give to Caesar the things that are Caesar's and to God the things that are God's.

25 When questioned about the resurrection from the dead, Jesus answered, When married persons rise from the dead, they neither marry nor are given in marriage, but are as the angels that are in heaven.

29-31 When asked about the first of all commandments, Jesus answered, The first of all the commandments is this, Hear, oh Israel; The Lord our God is one Lord, and you shall love the Lord your God with all your heart, and with all your soul, and with all your mind, and with all your strength. And the second is like it, You shall love your neighbor as yourself.

32 The scribe said to him, Well, Master, you have spoken the truth, for there is one God, and there is no other but you.

35-37 Jesus said to the people while he taught in the temple, How do the scribes conclude that Christ is the son of David? David himself said by the Holy Ghost, The LORD said to my Lord, Sit on my right hand until I make your enemies your footstool. David, therefore, called him Lord, so how is he then his son? (Jesus is rightfully claiming that he is God.)

Mark 13

5-6 Jesus talked to his disciples, Take care so no man deceives you. Many shall come in my name saying, I am Christ and shall deceive many.

13 You shall be hated by all men for my name's sake, but he who endures to the end shall be saved.

22-23 False Christs and false prophets shall rise and shall show signs and wonders to seduce you; if it were possible, even the elect. But take notice; I have foretold all things.

26-27 Then shall they see the Son of Man coming in the clouds with great power and glory. He shall send his angels and gather together his elect from the four winds, from the farthest part of the earth to the uttermost part of heaven.

31 Heaven and earth shall pass away, but my words shall not pass away.

32-33 Of that day and that hour no man knows, not the angels in heaven, nor the Son, only the Father. Take care. Watch and pray, for you know not when the time comes.

Mark 14 Christ and the cross event.

7 Jesus taught, You have the poor with you always, and whenever you will, you may do them good, but you do not always have me.

38 Watch and pray, so that you do not enter into temptation. The spirit truly is ready, but your flesh is weak.

60 The high priest stood up in the crowd and asked Jesus, Are you not going to answer? What is it these witnesses have against you?

61 But Jesus held his peace and answered nothing. Again the high priest asked him, Are you the Christ, the Son of the Blessed?

62 And Jesus said, I am, and you shall see the Son of Man sitting on the right hand of power and coming in the clouds of heaven.

Mark 15

2 Pilate asked Christ, Are you the King of the Jews? He answered, You said it.

14 Then Pilate said to the people, Why? What evil has he done? They cried out, Crucify him.

25 It was the third hour (9 AM), and they crucified him.

26 And on the cross it was written, THE KING OF THE JEWS.

34 At the ninth hour (3 PM) Jesus cried with a loud voice, saying, Eloi, Eloi, lama sabachthani? This interpreted says, My God, my God, why have you forsaken me?

37 Then Jesus cried with a loud voice and gave up his life.

38 And the veil of the temple was torn into two pieces, from the top to the bottom.

46 After the crucifixion they bought fine linen and took Christ down from the cross. They wrapped him in the linen, laid him in a sepulchre which was hewn out of a rock, and rolled a stone to cover the doorway.

Mark 16

6 An angel said to those who visited the grave, Be not frightened; you seek Jesus of Nazareth, who was crucified. He is risen. He is not here; behold the place where they laid him.

9 When Jesus had risen early the first day of the week, he appeared first to Mary Magdalene.

14-16 Afterward that, he appeared to the eleven disciples as they sat eating. He said to them, Go into all the world, and preach the gospel to every creature. He who believes and is baptized shall be saved, but he who believes not shall be damned.

19 After the Lord had spoken to them, he was received up into heaven and sat on the right hand of God.

Luke

Luke's gospel has a different perspective from Matthew, Mark, or John. .

Luke 1

32-33 Jesus shall be great and shall be called the Son of the Highest. The Lord God shall give to him the throne of his father David, and he shall reign over the house of Jacob forever. His kingdom shall have no end.

Luke 2

11 To you is born this day in the city of David a Savior who is Christ the Lord. 52 As Jesus grew up, he increased in wisdom and stature and in favor with God and man.

Luke 3

16 John answered, saying to those who followed him, I indeed baptize you with water, but one mightier than I comes, the laces of whose shoes I am not worthy to untie. He shall baptize you with the Holy Ghost and with fire.

Luke 4

8 Jesus answered Satan in the wilderness, Get behind me, Satan, for it is written, You shall worship the Lord your God, and him only shall you serve. 12 Jesus said to Satan, You shall not tempt the Lord your God. 43 Later, Jesus said to a crowd following him, I must preach the kingdom of God to other cities also; that is why I was sent.

Luke 5

10-11 Jesus said to Simon, the fisherman, Fear not; hereafter you shall catch men. And when they had brought their ships to land, they gave up everything and followed him.

Luke 6

27-31 Jesus taught, But I say, Love your enemies; do good to those who hate you; bless those who curse you, and pray for those who despitefully use you. And to him who hits you on one cheek, offer him the other. He who

takes away your coat, give him your sweater also. Give to every man who
asks of you, and of him who takes away your goods, ask not for them back.
As you would like men to do to you, do also to them.

32-34 If you love those who love you and do good to those who do good
to you, what thanks have you? Sinners also love those who love them and
do good to those who do good to them. If you lend to those from whom you
hope to collect, what thanks have you, for sinners also lend to sinners to
receive as much back again.

35-36 Love your enemies, and do good. Lend, hoping for nothing in
return. Your reward shall be great, and you shall be the children of the Most
High. Be merciful as your Father also is merciful.

37-38 Judge not and you shall not be judged; condemn not and you shall
not be condemned; forgive and you shall be forgiven. Give and it shall be
given to you, good measure, pressed down, shaken together, and running
over. With the same measure that you give, it shall be measured to you again.

40 The disciple is not above his master, but everyone who is perfect shall
be like his master.

41-42 Why look for the mote that is in your brother's eye and not discover
the beam that is in your own eye? How can you say to your brother, Let me
pull out the mote that is in your eye when you do not know that you have
a beam in your own eye? You hypocrite. First throw out the beam that is in
your own eye, and then you shall see clearly to pull out the mote that is in
your brother's eye.

43 A good tree does not produce corrupt fruit; neither does a corrupt tree
produce good fruit.

45 A good man, out of the good treasure of his heart, brings out that which
is good. An evil man, out of the evil treasure of his heart, brings out that
which is evil, for out of the abundance of his heart his mouth speaks.

Luke 9

2 Jesus sent his disciples to preach the kingdom of God and to heal the sick.

20 He said to them, Whom do you say that I am? Peter answering said,
You are the Christ sent by God.

23 He said to them, If any man will come after me, let him deny himself,
take up his cross daily, and follow me.

26 Whoever shall be ashamed of me and my words, of him shall the Son of
Man be ashamed when he shall come in his own glory, and in his Father's,
and in the holy angel's glory.

35 There came a voice out of the cloud, saying, This is my beloved Son;
hear him.

48 Jesus said to them, Whoever shall receive this child in my name receives

me, and whoever shall receive me receives him who sent me, for he who is least among you, the same shall be great.

59-60 Jesus said, Follow me, but the man said to him, Lord, allow me first to go and bury my father. Jesus said, Let the dead bury their dead; go and preach the kingdom of God.

62 Jesus said to him, No man having put his hand to the plow and looks back is fit for the kingdom of God.

Luke 10

2 Jesus said, The harvest truly is great, but the laborers are few. Pray to the Lord of the harvest, that he would send out laborers into his harvest.

5 Into whose house you enter, first say, Peace be to this house.

8-9 Into whose city you enter and they receive you, eat such things as are set before you. Heal the sick that are there and say to them, The kingdom of God is come close to you.

17 Seventy men returned again with joy saying, Lord, even the devils are subject to us through your name.

19 I give to you power to walk on serpents and scorpions and over all the power of the enemy, and nothing shall hurt you.

22 All things are delivered to me by my Father. No man knows who the Son is, but the Father, and who the Father is, but the Son, and him to whom the Son will reveal himself.

27 Jesus answered, You shall love the Lord your God with all your heart, soul, mind, and strength. And love your neighbor as yourself.

Luke 11

17 Jesus, knowing their thoughts taught, Every kingdom divided against itself is brought to ruin, and a house divided against itself falls.

23 He who is not with me is against me, and he who gathers not with me scatters.

34 The light of the body is the eye, so when your eye is single focused, your whole body is full of light, but when your eye is evil, your body also is full of darkness.

35 Take care that the light which you have is not really darkness.

Luke 12

3 Whatever you have spoken in darkness shall be heard in the light, and that which you have spoken in the ear in closets shall be proclaimed upon the housetops.

8 Whoever shall confess me before men, him shall the Son of Man also confess before the angels of God

9 He who denies me before men shall be denied before the angels of God.

10 Whoever shall speak a word against the Son of Man, it shall be forgiven him, but to him who blasphemes against the Holy Ghost it shall not be forgiven.

11-12 When they bring you to the synagogues to the judge, take no thought of how or what you shall say, for the Holy Ghost shall teach you in that same hour what you ought to say.

15 Jesus taught, Take notice of covetousness, for a man's life consists not in the abundance of the things which he possesses.

16-19 The ground of a certain rich man produced plentifully, so he thought to himself, What shall I do? I have no room to store my fruits? This I will do; I will pull down my barns and build greater, and there will I store all my fruits. Then I will say to my soul, Soul, you have much goods laid up for many years; take it easy, eat, drink, and be merry.

21 So is he who lays up treasure for himself and is not rich toward God.

23 Life is more than food, and the body is more than clothes.

28 If God clothes the grass, which is today in the field and tomorrow is thrown into the oven, how much more will he clothe you? Oh you of little faith.

29-31 Seek not what you shall eat or what you shall drink; neither have a doubtful mind. For all these things do the nations of the world seek after. Your Father knows that you have need of these things, but rather seek the kingdom of God and all these things shall be added to you.

33 Sell what you have and give offerings. Provide yourselves a treasure in heaven that fails not, where no thief approaches, neither do moths eat holes.

34 Where your treasure is, there will your heart be also.

49 I have come to send fire on the earth, but what will I do if it is already on fire?

51 Do you believe that I have came to give peace to the earth? I tell you, No. I came to divide it.

Luke 13

3 If you do not repent of your sins, you shall perish.

Luke 15

7 I say to you, There shall be more joy in heaven over one sinner who repents than over ninety and nine justified persons who need no repentance.

Luke 16

10 He who is faithful in little is also faithful in much, and he who is unjust in little is also unjust in much.

13 No servant can serve two masters, for either he will hate the one and love the other, or he will hold to the one and despise the other. You cannot serve God and wealth.

15 Jesus said to them, You justify yourselves before men, but God knows your hearts, for what you highly value among men is an abomination in the sight of God.

26 Between you and God there is a great gulf fixed, so that those who would try to go from here to God cannot bridge that gap.

Luke 17

1 Then Jesus said to his disciples, Sin will come, but great sorrow will come to him through whom they come!

2 Behold, the kingdom of God is within you.

Luke 18

16 Jesus said, Suffer the little children to come to me and forbid them not, for of such is the kingdom of God.

17 I say to you, Whoever shall not receive the kingdom of God as a little child shall in no way enter it.

25 It is easier for a camel to go through the eye of a needle than for a rich man to enter into the kingdom of God.

Luke 19

46 It is written, My house is a house of prayer, but you have made it a den of thieves.

Luke 20

25 Jesus said, Give to Caesar the things which are Caesar's and to God the things which are God's.

35-36 Those who are resurrected from the dead neither marry nor are given in marriage. Neither can they die any more, for they are equal to the angels and are children of God, being the children of the resurrection.

44 David, in the OLD TESTAMENT, was really calling Christ, LORD God. How is he then Christ's son?
(So, Christ is both LORD God and Christ the Son, equal in all attributes.)

Luke 21

34 Take notice of yourselves, unless at any time you overdo drinking and the cares of this life, and death overcomes you unawares.

Luke 22

69 Hereafter, the Son of Man shall sit on the right hand of the power of God.

Luke 24

47-48 Repentance and forgiveness of sins should be preached in Christ's name among all nations, beginning at Jerusalem.

John

God's Word speaks well for itself. It must have been almost indescribable to have been with Christ and listened to him teach. John's writings are so rich and powerful. They reveal the very beginning of creation. John fills our minds with words of truth that convict us of sin. It is a book of hope and expectancy. John makes solid the foundation of the OLD TESTAMENT.

The verses of John 1:1-5, below, destroys man's evolution theory. It is the only logical answer that can exist to explain our beginnings. God's immeasurable power is simply in his ability to speak, and his will is then accomplished. We have no right to question God's will, yet his perfect love allows it.

John 1

1-5 In the beginning was the Word, and the Word was with God, and the Word was God. The same was in the beginning with God. All things were made by him, and without him was nothing made. In him was life, and the life was the light of men. And the light shined in the darkness, and the darkness comprehended it not.
12-13 But as many as received him, to them he gave power to become

the sons of God, even to those who believe on his name, (Note the word "become". Belief must come before you become a child of God. You are not first a child of God, or you could not be adopted into God's family, which is God's only way for you and me to "become" a child of God.)

13 The new birth, born again, is not of blood, nor of the will of the flesh, nor of the will of man, but of God.

14 The Word became flesh and dwelt among us, and we beheld his glory, the glory as of the only begotten of the Father, full of grace and truth.

17 The law was given by Moses, but grace and truth came by Jesus Christ.

18 No man has seen God at any time, but the only begotten Son, Jesus Christ, has declared God to us.

29 The next day John saw Jesus coming to him and said, Behold the Lamb of God who takes away the sin of the world.

32 John testified saying, I saw the Holy Spirit descending from heaven like a dove, and it rested upon Christ.

33 I, John, knew him not, but God who sent me to baptize with water says, Upon whom you shall see the Spirit descending and remaining on him, the same is he who baptizes with the Holy Ghost.

34 I saw and give testimony that this Jesus is the Son of God.

36 Looking upon Jesus as he walked, John said, Behold the Lamb of God!

41 John found his brother Simon and said to him, We have found the Messiah, which is interpreted the Christ.

John 3

3 Jesus answered, Verily, verily, I say to you, Except a man be born again, he cannot enter the kingdom of God.

6 He who is born of the flesh is flesh, and he who is born of the Spirit is spirit.

7 Marvel not that I said to you, You must be born again.

13 No man has ascended up to heaven, but he who came down from heaven, even the Son of Man who is in heaven.

16 God so loved the world that he gave his only begotten Son, that whosoever believes in him should not perish, but have everlasting life. (This verse is the essence of the entire *Bible's* message. It can stand alone and explain God's complete plan of salvation to us. This is how simple it is. Yet, verse 19 shows us that man is the problem.)

17 For God sent not his Son into the world to condemn the world, but that the world through him might be saved.

18 He who believes on Christ is not condemned, but he who believes not is condemned already because he has not believed in the name of the only begotten Son of God.

19 This is the condemnation, that light has come into the world, and men

loved darkness rather than light because their deeds were evil.

20 Everyone who does evil hates the light; neither do they come to the light because their deeds will be exposed.

27 John answered and said, A man can receive nothing, except it is given him from heaven.

33 He who has received Christ's testimony has made his stand that God is true.

36 He who believes on the Son has everlasting life, and he who believes not the Son shall not see life, but the wrath of God is on him.

John 4

10 Jesus answered her, If you knew the gift of God and who it is who says to you, Give me a drink, you would have asked of him, and he would have given you living water.

14 Whoever drinks of the water that I shall give him shall never thirst, but the water that I give shall be in him a well of water springing up into everlasting life.

23 The hour comes, and now is, when true worshipers shall worship the Father in spirit and in truth.

24 God is a Spirit, and those who worship him must worship him in spirit and in truth.

34 Jesus said to them, My desire is to do the will of God who sent me and to finish his work.

35 Say not, There are yet four months and then comes the harvest. I say to you, Lift up your eyes and look at the fields, for they are white already to harvest.

42 The Samaritan said to the woman, Now we believe, not because of what you said, for we have heard him ourselves and know that this is indeed the Christ, the Savior of the world.

John 5

13 He who was healed knew not who healed him, for Jesus had gone away.

19 Jesus spoke, I say to you, The Son can do nothing of himself, but what he sees the Father do, for whatever things he does, the Son also does.

21 As the Father raises up the dead and gives them life, even so the Son gives life to whom he will.

22 The Father judges no man but has committed all judgment to the Son.

24 I say, He who hears my Word and believes on God who sent me has everlasting life. He shall not come into condemnation but is passed from death to life.

27 God has given Christ the authority to execute judgment because he is the Son of Man.

29 They shall come out of the grave, those who have done good to the resurrection of life, and those who have done evil to the resurrection of damnation.

John 6

29 Jesus answered, This is the work of God, that you believe me whom God has sent.

35 Jesus mysteriously spoke, I am the bread of life. He who comes to me shall never hunger, and he who believes in me shall never thirst.

37 All those whom the Father gives me shall come to me, and those who come to me I will in no way cast out.

47 I say to you, He who believes in me has everlasting life.

51 I am the living bread who came down from heaven. If any man eats of this bread, he shall live forever, The bread that I will give is my flesh, which I will give for the life of the world.

53-54 Then Jesus continued, Unless you eat the flesh of the Son of Man and drink his blood, you have no life in you. Whoever eats my flesh and drinks my blood has eternal life, and I will raise him up at the last day.

56-57 He who eats my flesh and drinks my blood, dwells in me, and I in him. The living Father has sent me, and I live by the Father, so he who eats bread in remembrance of me shall live his life me.

58 I am that bread which came down from heaven, not as your forefathers did eat manna in the wilderness and are now dead. He who eats of my bread shall live forever.

63 It is the Spirit who gives life. The flesh profits nothing. The words that I speak to you are Spirit and life.

John 7

16 Jesus answered, My doctrine is not mine, but it is his who sent me.

17 If any man will do his will, he shall know about the doctrine, whether it is of God, or whether I speak of myself.

18 He who speaks of himself seeks his own glory, but he who seeks God's glory, which sent me, the same is true, and no unrighteousness is in him.

38 He who believes on me, as the scripture says, Out of him shall flow rivers of living water.

42 Has not the scripture said, Christ comes through the seed of David and out of the town of Bethlehem where David was?

John 8

1, 12 Jesus went to the Mount of Olives and spoke, I am the light of the world; he who follows me shall not walk in darkness but shall have the light of life.

23-24 Jesus said, You are from earth; I am from heaven. You are of this world; I am not of this world. I say to you that you shall die in your sins, for if you believe not that I am God, you shall die in your sins.

28 Then said Jesus, When you have lifted up the Son of Man, then shall you know that I am God and that I do nothing of myself.

31 Then said Jesus to those Jews who believed in him, If you continue in my Word, then you are my disciples indeed.

32 You shall know the truth, and the truth shall make you free.

34 Jesus answered, I say to you, Whoever commits sin is the servant of sin.

35 The servant stays not in the house forever, but the Son is here forever.

36 If the Son shall make you free, you shall be free indeed.

46-47 Who of you convicts me of sin? I speak the truth, so why do you not believe me? He who is of God hears God's words, but you do not hear them because you are not of God.

51 I say to you, If a man keeps my sayings, he shall never see death.

55 You have not known God, but I know him. If I should say, I know him not, I shall be a liar like you, but I know him and keep his words.

58 Jesus said to them, Before Abraham was, I am.

John 9

5 As long as I am in the world, I am the light of the world.

31 We know that God does not hear sinners, but if any man is a worshiper of God and does his will, God hears him.

John 10

9 I am the door. If any man enters in by me, he shall be saved and go in and out and find pasture.

27-28 My sheep hear my voice; I know them, and they follow me. I give to them eternal life, and they shall never perish; neither shall any man pluck them out of my hand.

30 I and my Father are one.

John 11

25-26 Jesus said to the woman, I am the resurrection and the life; he who believes in me, if he were dead, yet shall he live. Whoever lives and believes in me shall never die. Do you believe?

John 12

25 He who loves his life shall lose it, and he who hates his life in this world shall keep it to life eternal.

26 If any man serves me, let him follow me. Where I am there shall my servant be. If any man serves me, my Father will honor him.

32 If I be lifted up from the earth, I will draw all men to me.

35-36 Then Jesus said to them, Yet, for a little while is my light with you. Walk while you have that light before darkness comes upon you, for he who walks in darkness knows not where he goes. While you have light, believe in the light, so you may be the children of that light. Then Jesus departed and hid himself from them.

46 I am the light of the world; whoever believes in me should not remain in darkness.

48 He who rejects me and receives not my words has one who judges him. The words that I have spoken shall judge him in the last day.

John 14

1 Let not your heart be troubled. You believe in God; believe also in me.

6 Jesus said, I am the way, the truth, and the life; no man comes to the Father but by me.

11 Believe me, I am in the Father and the Father is in me. Or else believe me for the very works I do to redeem you.

12 I say to you, Believe in me. The works that I do shall you do also, and greater works than these shall you do because I go to my Father.

13 Whatever you shall ask in my name, that will I do, that the Father may be glorified in the Son.

15 If you love me, keep my commandments.

16-17 I will pray to the Father, and he shall give you the Comforter, who will stay with you forever. The Comforter is the Spirit of truth, whom the world cannot receive because it sees him not, nor knows him. But you know him, for he lives with you and shall be in you.

21 He who has my commandments and keeps them shall be loved by my Father. I will love him and will come to him.

23 Jesus answered and said to him, If a man loves me, he will keep my words; my Father will love him, and we will come to him and make our home with him.

26 The Father will send in my name, the Comforter, who is the Holy Ghost, to teach you all things and bring all things that I have taught you to your remembrance.

John 15

10 If you keep my commandments, you shall abide in my love, even as I have kept my Father's commandments and abide in his love.

13-14 Greater love has no man than this, than to lay down his life for his friends. You are my friends if you do what I command you.

16 You have not chosen me, but I have chosen you that you should go and bring forth fruit, and that your fruit should remain. So, whatever you shall ask of the Father in my name, he may give you.

17 These things I command that you love one another.

23 He who hates me hates my Father also.

24-25 I have done the miracles no other man has done. Men have seen and hated me and my Father, so that the Word might be fulfilled that is written in their law. They hated me without a cause.

26 When the Comforter comes, whom I will send to you from the Father, he shall testify of me.

John 16

9 Jesus clearly taught, The world's sin is that it refuses to believe in me.

10 Your righteousness is obtainable because I go to my Father.

13 When the Spirit of truth has come, he will guide you into all truth, for the Holy Spirit shall not speak of himself, but whatever he hears, that shall he speak, and he will show you things to come.

24 Until now, you have asked nothing in my name; ask and you shall receive that your joy may be full.

John 17

3 This is life eternal. Know God, the only true God and Jesus Christ, whom he has sent.

17 God, sanctify them through your truth, for your Word is truth.

John 18

37 Pilate said to Christ, prior to his crucifixion, Are you a king then? Jesus answered, You say that I am a king. To this end was I born, and for this cause I came into the world that I should give witness to the truth. Everyone who is of the truth hears my voice.

John 20

23 Those sins you forgive, they are forgiven them, and those sins you do not forgive, they are not forgiven them.

25 After Christ was crucified on the cross and risen from the dead, the other disciples said to Thomas, We have seen the LORD! But Thomas said to them, Unless I shall see Christ's hands, put my fingers on those nail prints, and put my hand into his side, I will not believe.

27 Christ said to Thomas when they met later, Reach your finger here and look at my hands; reach your hand here and put it into my side. Be not faithless, but believe.

28 Then Thomas answered Jesus, My LORD and my God!

29 Jesus did not rebuke him for saying he was God. He said, Blessed are those who have not seen and yet have believed.

31 John wrote, These things are written that you might believe that Jesus is the Christ, the Son of God, and that by believing you may have life through his name.

John 21

18 Jesus said to Peter prior to Christ's ascension to heaven, Now I say to you, When you were young, you clothed yourself and walked where you would, but when you become old, you shall stretch out your hands, and God shall hold you and carry you where you would not choose to go.

19 This signified by what death Peter would later glorify God. And when Christ had spoken this, he said to him, Follow me.

24 John wrote these things, and we know that his testimony is true.

25 There are many other things which Jesus did, and if they should all be written, I suppose that even the world itself could not contain the books that should be written. Amen. (Jesus is now preparing a place in heaven for all who will believe that Christ is our Emmanuel,)

Acts

This book is written by Luke, a doctor and friend of Paul, and is about God's Holy Spirit being left with man. The Holy Spirit teaches and convicts us of our sins. When we are convicted, it is up to us to decide to follow after Christ's righteousness or continue to be self-centered and follow temptation and sin.

Acts 2

4 They were all filled with the Holy Ghost and began to speak with other tongues (languages) as the Spirit gave them.

17 It shall come to be in the last days, says God, I will pour out my Spirit upon all flesh, and your sons and your daughters shall prophesy; your young men shall see visions, and your old men shall dream dreams.

18-21 On my servants and on my handmaidens I will pour out my Spirit in those days, and they shall prophesy. And I will show wonders in heaven above and signs on the earth below: blood, fire, and smoke. The sun shall be turned into darkness and the moon into blood before the great and notable day when the Lord returns. And it shall happen that whoever shall call on the name of the Lord shall be saved.

32 God has raised up Jesus, and all of us are witnesses for Christ.

36 Therefore, let all of Israel know undoubtedly that God has made this same Jesus, whom you have crucified, both Lord and Christ.

37-38 Now when the people heard this, they were pricked in their heart and said to Peter and the rest of the apostles, Men and brethren, what shall we do? Then Peter said to them, Repent and be baptized everyone of you in the name of Jesus Christ for the remission of sins, and you shall receive the gift of the Holy Ghost.

Acts 3

19 Repent and be converted, so that your sins may be gone when the eternal time of refreshing shall come, and we are in the presence of the Lord.

Acts 4

12 There is no salvation in any other, for there is no other name under heaven given to men whereby we can be saved.

Acts 15

11 We believe it is through the grace of the LORD Jesus Christ that we shall be saved.

Acts 16

30-31 Believe in the Lord Jesus Christ, and you shall be saved, and your house. And they spoke the Word of the Lord to him and to all who were in his house.

Acts 17

24-25 God made the world and all things in it. We see that he is Lord of heaven and earth; he dwells not in temples made with hands. Neither is he worshiped with men's hands as though he needed anything. He gives to every person life, breath, and all things. (Acts 17:25 explains, in part, how God has existed from eternity past and had no beginning. He says he has no needs and can satisfy every need. That fact is mind boggling. In Ecclesiastes 3:11, God says he has put the concept of time in man's heart, so that man can discover God's plans for man from man's beginnings on into eternity. Not from God's beginning, since there is none.)

(Right now there is a fork in the road. One path leads to eternal Hell, and the other leads to eternal Heaven and into the very presence of God, Christ and the Holy Spirit. Your choice of path is so important.)

26 Christ has made of one blood all nations of men to dwell on all the earth, and he has determined the times before they happen and the limits of their reach.
31 God has appointed a day when he will judge the world in righteousness by Christ, whom he has ordained. Therefore, God has given assurance to all men that he has raised Christ from the dead.

Acts 19

5-6 When the people heard this, they were baptized in the name of the Lord Jesus. And when Paul had laid his hands upon them, the Holy Ghost came on them, and they spoke with tongues and prophesied.

Acts 20

28 Take notice to yourselves and the believers. The Holy Ghost has made you overseers, to preach Christ to the church of God, which he purchased with his own blood.
30 Other men shall arise, speaking dishonest things to draw away disciples after themselves.
32 I commend you to God and to the Word of his grace. His Word is able to build you up to give you an inheritance among all those who are sanctified, who are made holy.
35 I have shown you all things: How to work to support the weak and how to remember the words of the Lord Jesus. He said, It is more blessed to give than to receive.

Acts 23

5 It is written, You shall not speak evil of the ruler of your people.

Acts 24

15 Have hope in God, there shall be a resurrection of the dead, both of the just and unjust.

Romans

Romans is written by the Apostle Paul. Romans is about God's grace that extends his absolute holiness to sinful man through the death of Christ to pay our sin debt. Faith is believing that this is true. Christ then becomes our Advocate before our holy God. In Romans, we find the "Roman Road." It shows clear steps to salvation by God's grace. Memorize these verses and share them with others. These are found on page 162, near the end of this book.

The book of Romans assures us that it is by faith in Christ and not in the law of doing works of righteousness that we are saved.

Romans 1

3-5 Christ was born out of the lineage of David (OLD TESTAMENT), according to the flesh. He is declared to be the Son of God with power, according to the Spirit of Holiness by his resurrection from the dead, by whom we have received grace, for obedience to the faith in his name.
7 Paul wrote, To all who are in Rome, loved by God and called to be saints, grace to you and peace from God our Father and the Lord Jesus Christ.
16-17 I am not ashamed of the gospel of Christ, for it is the power of God to salvation, to everyone who believes, to the Jew first and also to the Greek. In the Gospel is the righteousness of God revealed from faith to faith. It is written, The just shall live by faith.
18 The wrath of God is revealed from heaven against all ungodliness and unrighteousness of men, who hold the truth in unrighteousness.
23 Man has changed the glory of the incorruptible God into images made like corruptible man, birds, animals, and creeping things.
24 Therefore, God gave them up to uncleanness through the lusts of their own hearts, to dishonor their own bodies between themselves.
26-27 God gave these men up to vile affections, for even their women did change the natural use of their bodies into that which is against nature.

Likewise also the men, leaving the natural use of the woman. They burned with lust one toward another, men with men, working that which is ungodly and receiving in themselves that penalty for their error which was due them.

Romans 2

2 We are sure that the judgment of God is according to truth; it is against those who judge not by truth.

4 The goodness of God leads us to repentance.

5-6 Because you harden your heart against God, God will give to every man according to his deeds.

11 There is no partiality of persons with God.

12 Those who have sinned without the law shall also perish without the law, and those who have sinned in the law shall be judged by the law.

14 When the Gentiles, who do not have the law, do by nature the things contained in the law, these are a law to themselves.

15 Men show the work of the law written in their hearts; their conscience also bears witness. Even their thoughts accuse or excuse one another.

16 On judgment day God shall judge the secrets of men by Jesus Christ, according to the gospel.

21 You who teach others, do you not also teach yourself? You who preach that a man should not steal, do you steal?

26 Therefore, if the uncircumcised keep the righteousness of the law, shall not his uncircumcision be counted to him for circumcision?

29 He is a Jew, who is one inwardly, and circumcision is that of the heart in the spirit, and not in the letter, whose praise is not of men but of God.

Romans 3

10 It is written, There is none righteous. No, not one.

19 Now we know that what the law says, it says to those who are under the law, that every mouth may be shut, and all the world may become guilty before God.

20 By keeping the law, no person is justified in God's sight, for by the law comes the knowledge of sin.

21 The righteousness of God is clear without the law, yet it is witnessed to by the law and the prophets.

22 The righteousness of God, which is by faith in Jesus Christ, is to all and upon all persons who believe.

23 All have sinned and come short of the glory of God.

25 God has made Christ to be a propitiation (atonement) through faith in his blood. He declares his righteousness for the remission of sins that are past.

26 I say about Christ's righteousness, that Christ is just and the justifier of those who believe in him.

28 We conclude that a man is justified by faith, without keeping the law.

30 Seeing it is one God, he shall justify circumcisions by faith and the uncircumcised through faith.

31 Do we make void the law through faith? God forbid; we actually establish the law.

Romans 4

3 What does the scripture say? It says, Abraham believed God, and it was counted to him for righteousness.

5 To him who does no good works but believes on him who justifies the ungodly, his faith is counted to him for righteousness.

15 The law results in punishment, for where there is no law to break, there is no sin.

16 Therefore, it is about faith, that it might be by grace, so that the promise might be sure to all of Abraham's seed, not to those only who keep the law, but to those also who are of the faith of Abraham. He is the father of us all.

21-22 I am fully persuaded that what God has promised, he is able to do. Therefore, it was imputed to Abraham for righteousness.

24-25 Righteousness was for us also, to whom it shall be imputed if we believe that God raised up Jesus our Lord from the dead. He was crucified for our offenses and was raised again for our justification.

Romans 5

This is a chapter of contrasts. It is about the two paths leading from our fork in the road. Who do you say that Christ is?

1-5 Therefore, being justified by faith, we have peace with God through our Lord Jesus Christ. By Christ we have access by faith into this grace wherein we stand and rejoice in the hope of the glory of God. And not only that, but we glory in tribulations also, knowing that tribulation works patience, and patience, experience, and experience, hope. Hope causes no shame because the love of God is in our hearts by the Holy Ghost, who resides in us.

8 God extends his love toward us, in that while we were yet sinners, Christ died for us.

9 Much more then, being now justified by his blood, we shall be saved from God's anger by Christ.

11 And not only that, but we have joy in God through our Lord Jesus

Christ, by whom we have now received the atonement.

12 By one man, Adam, sin entered into the world causing death, so death has passed on to all men, for all men have sinned.

13 Before the law was given, sin was in the world, but sin is not imputed when there is no law.

14 Nevertheless, death exists from Adam to Moses, even over those who had not sinned just like Adam's sin. Adam was an opposite type of Christ who was to come. (Adam leads us to death, and Christ leads us to life eternal.)

15 Not like the offense of Adam, there is this free gift. For if through the offense of Adam, many are dead, much more is the grace of God and his free gift by grace, which is by one man, Jesus Christ. It has expanded to many.

16 And not as it was by Adam who sinned, so is this gift, for the judgment was by Adam to condemnation, but the free gift is for many offenses to justification.

18 Therefore, as the offense of Adam's judgment came upon all men to condemnation by the righteousness of Christ, the free gift came upon all men to justification of life.

20 Moreover, the law came, that the offense might be exposed. But where sin abounded, grace did much more abound.

Romans 6

4 We are buried with Christ by baptism into death, but as Christ was raised up from the dead by the glory of the Father, even so we also should walk in new life.

7 He who is dead is freed from sin.

8 If we are dead with Christ, we believe that we shall also live with him.

12 Let no sin reign in your mortal body; you should not obey the lusts of it.

13 Neither yield your body's parts as instruments of unrighteousness to sin, but yield yourselves to God as those who are alive from the dead and your body as an instrument of righteousness to God.

23 The wages of sin is death, but the gift of God is eternal life through Jesus Christ our Lord.

Romans 7

15 That which I do, I should not do, but what I hate, that I do.

22-25 I delight in the law of God after the inward man, but I see another law in myself, warring against the law of my mind and bringing me into captivity to the law of sin which is in myself. Oh, wicked man that I am! Who shall deliver me from this death? I thank God through Jesus Christ our

Lord. So with my mind I serve the law of God, but with the flesh I serve the law of sin.

Romans 8

1 There is now no condemnation for those who are in Christ Jesus, who walk not after the flesh, but after the Spirit.

2 The law of the Spirit of life in Christ Jesus has made me free from the law of sin and death.

6 To be carnally minded is death, but to be spiritually minded is life and peace.

7 The carnal mind is against God, for it is not subject to the law of God.

9 You are not in the flesh, but you are in the Spirit if the Spirit of God dwells in you. Now, if any man does not have the Spirit of Christ in him, he is none of Christ's.

11 If the Spirit of God, who raised up Jesus from the dead, dwells in you, he who raised up Christ from the dead shall also restore your mortal bodies by his Spirit who dwells in you.

14 As many as are led by the Spirit of God, they are the sons of God.

15 You have not received the spirit of bondage to have fear, but you have received the Spirit of adoption, whereby we cry, Abba, Father.

16-17 The Holy Spirit itself bears witness with our spirit that we are the children of God. If children, then we are heirs, heirs of God and joint-heirs with Christ if we suffer with him, by bearing our own cross of trials and persecution, that we may be glorified together with him.

19 Creation expectantly waits for the revealing of the sons of God.

21 The creation shall be delivered from the bondage of sin into that glorious liberty of the children of God.

22-23 We know that the whole creation groans and suffers in pain until now. Not only they, but ourselves also, who have the first fruits of the Spirit; even we ourselves groan within ourselves waiting for the adoption and redemption of our body.

26 The Spirit helps our weaknesses, for we know not what we should pray for, but the Spirit itself makes intercession for us with groanings which cannot be verbalized.

28 We know that all things work together for good to those who love God, to those who are called according to his purpose.

31 What shall we then say to these things? If God be for us, who can be against us?

32 He who spared not his own Son, but delivered him up for us all, he freely gives us all things.

37 No, in all these things we are more than conquerors through him who loved us.

38 I am persuaded that neither death, life, angels, principalities, powers, things present, nor things to come can separate us from the love of God.

Romans 9

15-16 God said to Moses, I will have mercy on whom I will have mercy, and I will have compassion on whom I will have compassion. So it is God who shows mercy.

Romans 10

4 Christ is the end of the law; he gives righteousness to everyone who believes.
9-10 If you confess with your mouth the Lord Jesus and believe in your heart that God has raised him from the dead, you shall be saved. For with the heart man believes for righteousness, and with the mouth confession is made for salvation.
13 Whoever shall call upon the name of the Lord shall be saved.
14 How then shall they call on him in whom they have not believed? And how shall they believe in him of whom they have not heard? And how shall they hear without a preacher?
15 How shall they preach, except they be sent? As it is written, How beautiful are the feet of those who preach the gospel of peace and bring glad tidings of good things!
17 So then faith comes by hearing, and hearing by the Word of God.

Romans 11

17 Some of the branches have been broken off, and you, being a wild olive shoot, have been grafted in among the others and now share in the life of Christ.
19 Due to unbelief, branches were broken off so that I could be grafted in.
23 If they do not remain in unbelief, they will be grafted in, for God is able to graft them in again.
24 If you were cut out of an olive tree that is wild by nature, and you were grafted into a cultivated olive tree, how much more readily will these, the natural branches, be grafted into their own olive tree!
25 I would not want you to be ignorant of this mystery. Blindness in part has happened to Israel until the fullness of the Gentiles comes in.
32 God has allowed all their unbelief, that he might have mercy upon all.
33 Oh the depth and riches of the wisdom and knowledge of God! How unsearchable are his judgments, and his ways cannot be found out!
34-35 Who has known the mind of the Lord, or who has been his Counselor?

36 Of Him, through Him, and to Him are all things, to whom be glory forever. Amen.

Romans 12

1 I ask you, by the mercies of God, that you present your bodies a living sacrifice, holy and acceptable to God, which is reasonable to ask.
2 You should not be conformed to this world, but be transformed by the renewing of your mind, that you may prove what is the good, acceptable, and perfect will of God.
3 Man should not think of himself more highly than he ought, but he should think soberly, according as God has given to every man the measure of faith.
4-5 As we have many members in one body, so we, being many, are one body in Christ, and everyone is a member with the other.
6-8 We have gifts differing according to the grace that is given to us. If we have the gift of prophecy, let us prophesy according to our proportion of faith. If ministry, let us wait on our ministering; he who teaches, on teaching; he who exhorts, on exhortation. He who gives, let him do it with simplicity; he who rules, do it with caring; he who shows mercy, do it with cheerfulness.
9 Let love no be hidden. Hate that which is evil; hold on to that which is good.
10 Be loving one to another with brotherly love, in honor preferring one another.
12 Be rejoicing in hope, be patient in troubles, and be constant in prayer.
13 When distributing to the necessity of saints, be hospitable.
14 Bless those who persecute you; bless and do not curse.
15 Rejoice with those who rejoice and weep with those who weep.
16 Be of the same mind one toward another. Do not think highly of things, but stoop down to men of low estate. Be not boastful in your own ego.
17-18 Pay back no man evil for evil. Provide things honest in the sight of all men. If it is possible, as much as you can, live peaceably with all men.
19 Do not take revenge, but leave that to God, for it is written, Vengeance is mine; I will repay, says the Lord.
20 If your enemy is hungry, feed him; if he thirsts, give him drink. By doing that, you heap coals of fire on his head.
21 Be not overcome by evil, but overcome evil with good.

Romans 13

2 Whoever resists the authorities resists the ordinance of God, and those who resist shall receive damnation.

8 Owe no man anything, but love one another, for he who loves has fulfilled God's law.

9-10 You shall not commit adultery; you shall not kill, steal, nor give a false witness. You shall not covet, and if there be any other commandment, it is this: You shall love your neighbor as yourself. Love does not hurt his neighbor; love is the fulfilling of God's law.

11 It is the time to awake out of sleep, for now is our salvation nearer than when we first believed.

12 The night is about gone; the day is here. Let us throw off the works of evil, and let us protect ourselves with God's Word.

13-14 Let us walk honestly, not in rioting and drunkenness, not in strife and envying, but be like the Lord Jesus Christ. Make no provision to fulfil our own lusts.

Romans 15

2-3 Let everyone of us please our neighbor for his good. For even Christ pleased not himself. It is written, The rebuke of those who rebuke you fell on me, (Christ).

5 Now the God of patience and consolation grant you to be like-minded toward one another according to Christ Jesus.

7 Receive one another as Christ also received us to the glory of God.

8 Jesus Christ was a minister of the circumcision for the truth of God to confirm the promises made to your forefathers.

11 Praise the Lord, all you Gentiles, and praise him, everyone.

13 May the God of hope fill you with all joy and give you peace in believing, that you may have great hope through the power of the Holy Spirit.

33 Now may the God of peace be with you all. Amen.

Romans 16

17-18 Separate from those who cause divisions and offenses that are against the doctrines you have learned. Avoid them, for they do not serve the Lord Jesus Christ, but themselves.

25 Jesus has the power to save you, which is told you by my gospel and preaching of Jesus Christ, according to revelations which were kept secret since the world began.

27 To the only wise God, be glory through Jesus Christ forever. Amen.

God has done all to save man from his sin, yet the cross is foolishness
to the majority of mankind. If salvation were by keeping laws unbroken,
nobody would be saved, but God made it so simple-- "It is by grace that we
are saved through faith!" The desire to be controlled by sin appeals to the
majority of people because they want to forget God's ways and even desire
to become gods by man's rules and self-pride.

1 Corinthians 1

7 Lack no spiritual gift while waiting for the second coming of our Lord
Jesus Christ.
18 The preaching of the cross is foolishness to those who perish, but to us
who are saved it is the power of God.
25 The foolishness of God is wiser than men, and the weakness of God is
stronger than men.

1 Corinthians 2

9-10 It is written, Eye has not seen, nor ear heard; neither has it entered
into the heart of man the things which God has prepared for those who love
him. But God has revealed them to us by his Spirit, for the Spirit searches
all things; yes, the deep things of God.

1 Corinthians 3

11 No other foundation can any man lay than that which is laid, which is
Christ Jesus.
16 Know that you are the temple of God and that the Spirit of God dwells
in you.
17 If any man defiles the temple of God, God shall destroy him, for the
temple of God, who is in you, is holy.

1 Corinthians 4

20 The kingdom of God is not just words, but it is living power.

1 Corinthians 5

9 I wrote to you in an epistle, do not have relationships with fornicators.

12 How can I judge those who are not believers? Do you not judge those who are believers?

1 Corinthians 6

1 How is it that you who have a matter against another person and go to law before the unjust and not before the saints?
2 Do you not know that the saints shall judge the world? If the world shall be judged by you, are you unworthy to judge the smallest matters?
16 What, do you not know that he that is joined to a harlot is one body? Know that these two become one flesh.
18 Flee fornication. Every other sin that a man does is outside the body, but he who commits fornication sins against his own body.
19 What, do you not know that your body is the temple of the Holy Ghost who is in you, given by God? You are not your own.
12 When you sin against believers, and it hurts them, you sin against Christ.

1 Corinthians 9

16 When I preach the gospel, I have nothing that I can take credit for, but if I do not preach the gospel, I am troubled!
22 To the weak person I sympathize, so I might win him to Christ. In like manner, I try to relate to all men in some way, that I might by all means save some.
24 Do you not know that all who are in the race run, but it is only one who receives the prize? So run the race, so that you might win the prize.

1 Corinthians 10

12 Let him who thinks he stands, beware. He just may fall.
13 There is no temptation that you will experience that is not common to all mankind, but God is faithful. He will not allow you to be tempted beyond what you are able to resist. God will make a way of escape, so that you can overcome it.
21 You cannot drink the cup of the Lord and the cup of devils; you cannot be partakers of the Lord's table and of the table of devils.
31 Whether you eat, or drink, or whatever you do, do all to the glory of God.

1 Corinthians 11

3 I would have you know that the head of every man is Christ, and the head of the woman is the man, and the head of Christ is God.

7 A man should not cover his head; he is the image and glory of God, but the woman is the glory of the man.

8 Man was not made from the woman, but the woman was made from the man.

9 Man was not created for the woman, but the woman was created for the man.

23 I have received from the Lord what I delivered to you, that the Lord Jesus, the same night in which he was betrayed, took bread and broke it.

27 Christ said, Whoever shall eat of this bread and drink of this cup of the Lord unworthily shall be guilty of rejecting the body and blood of the Lord.

32 As believers, when we are judged, we are corrected by the Lord; we are not condemned with the world.

1 Corinthians 12

4 There are different gifts, but the same Spirit.

7 The displaying of the Spirit is given to every man to profit many.

18 God has put the members that are in the body where it pleases him.

27 You are the body of Christ and members in particular.

1 Corinthians 13

2 Though I have the gift of prophecy and understand all mysteries and all knowledge, and though I have all faith, so that I could remove mountains and have not charity, I am nothing.

4 Charity suffers long and is kind. It does not envy nor boast.

7 Charity endures all things, believes all things, and hopes all things.

11 When I was a child, I spoke as a child. I understood as a child, and I thought as a child, but when I became a man, I put away my childish things.

12 Now we see through a glass darkly, but then face to face; now I know in part, but then I shall know even as I am known.

13 Now abide faith, hope, and love, but the greatest of these is love.

1 Corinthians 14

9 Except you speak words that are easy to understand, how shall it be known what is spoken?

13 Let him who speaks in an unknown language pray that he may interpret it.

16 When you bless with the spirit, how shall he and other unlearned persons say, Amen to your giving of thanks, seeing that he understands not what you said?

33 God is not the author of confusion, but of peace.

39-40 Desire to prophesy, and do not forbid believers from speaking in tongues. Let all things be done decently and in order.

1 Corinthians 15

10 By the grace of God I am what I am, and God's grace which was bestowed upon me was not in vain.

20 Now Christ is risen from the dead and become the first fruits of those who slept.

23 Every man in his own order. Christ is the first fruits; afterwards come those who are Christ's at his coming.

45 It is written, The first man Adam was made a living soul; the last Adam was made a life-giving Spirit.

50 Flesh and blood cannot inherit the kingdom of God; neither does corruption inherit incorruption.

53 This corruption must put on incorruption, and this mortal must put on immortality.

56-57 The sting of death is sin, and the strength of sin is the law. But thanks be to God. He gives us the victory through our Lord Jesus Christ.

58 Therefore, my fellow believers, be steadfast, unmovable, and always abounding in the work of the Lord. Know that your labor is not in vain in the Lord.

1 Corinthians 16

22 If any man does not love the Lord Jesus Christ, let him be cursed.

2 Corinthians

Sin puts us under control of the Devil, but Christ offers true freedom from now to all eternity. All of God's goodness can be ours.

2 Corinthians 1

2 Grace be to you and peace from God our Father and from the Lord Jesus Christ.

3 Blessed be God, who is the Father of our Lord Jesus Christ, the Father of mercies, and the God of all comfort.

4 He comforts us in all our sufferings, so that we may be able to comfort those who are in trouble, by the comfort which we ourselves have been comforted by God.

5 As the sufferings of Christ are many in us, so our comfort is great in Christ.

19-20 The Son of God, Jesus Christ, who we preached among you, was not just yes and no, but in him was yes alone. For all the promises of God in Christ are positive and to the glory of God.

2 Corinthians 3

17 Now the Lord is that Spirit, and where the Spirit of the Lord is, there is liberty.

2 Corinthians 4

3 If our gospel is hidden, it is hidden to those who are lost.
4 Satan, the god of this world, has blinded the minds of those who do not believe, if not, the light of the glorious gospel of Christ, who is the image of God, would shine on them.
6 It is God who commanded the light to shine out of darkness to show the light of the knowledge of the glory of God in the face of Jesus Christ.
8-9 We are troubled on every side, yet not distressed; we are perplexed, but not in despair. We are persecuted, but not forsaken, cast down, but not destroyed.
11-12 We who live are always delivered to death for the purposes of Jesus, so that the life of Jesus might be seen by others in our daily lives.

2 Corinthians 5

1 We know that if our body, which is God's tabernacle, died, we have a new tabernacle of God, not made with hands, that is eternal in the heavens.
9 We labor, whether it results in life or death, so that we may be accepted by Christ.
10 One day we all must appear before the judgment seat of Christ so that everyone may give account for the things done in this life, whether it was good or bad.
17 Therefore, if any man be in Christ, he is a new creature; old things are passed away. Behold, all things become new.
19 God was in Christ, reconciling the world to himself. He was not attributing the world's sins to God and Christ. He has charged us to tell of his Word of reconciliation.
20 We are ambassadors for Christ; we pray in Christ's name that you become reconciled to God.
21 God has made Christ to be sin for us who knew no sin, that we might be made the righteousness of God in him.

2 Corinthians 6

14 Be not unequally tied together with unbelievers, for what fellowship has righteousness with unrighteousness, and what in common has light with darkness?
15 What in common has Christ with the Devil, or in what part has the believer with an unbeliever?
17 Therefore, come out from among them and be separate, says the Lord; Touch not the unclean things, and I will receive you.

2 Corinthians 7

1 Having these promises, let us cleanse ourselves from all filthiness of our flesh and spirit, perfecting holiness in the fear of God.
10 Godly sorrow leads to repentance and salvation; sin is not to be repeated. The sorrow of the world leads to death.

2 Corinthians 9

7 Every man's offering reflects what is in his heart, so let him give, not grudgingly or out of necessity because God loves a cheerful giver.
9 It is written about Christ, he has spread abroad; he has given to the poor, and his righteousness remains forever.

2 Corinthians 11

14 Do not marvel that Satan himself is transformed into an angel of light to deceive.

2 Corinthians 12

9 Christ said to me, My grace is sufficient for you; my strength is made perfect in weakness. So I most gladly glory in my weaknesses, that the power of Christ may rest upon me.

2 Corinthians 13

1 This is the third time I am coming to you. By the mouth of two or three witnesses shall every word be established.
5 Examine yourselves, whether you are in the faith; prove yourselves. Know that you are not your own; know that Jesus Christ is in you.
11 Be perfect, and be of good comfort; be of one mind; live in peace, and

the God of love and peace shall be with you.

12 Greet one another with a holy kiss.

14 May the grace of the Lord Jesus Christ, the love of God, and the fellowship of the Holy Spirit be with you all. Amen.

Galatians

Galatians is a book about salvation by grace. Read how grace makes you right before the throne of holy God through Jesus Christ.

Galatians 1

4 Jesus sacrificed himself for our sins, delivering us from this present evil world, according to the will of God our Father.

5 To whom be glory forever and ever. Amen.

8 If we or an angel from heaven preach any other gospel to you than that which we have preached to you, let him be cursed.

Galatians 2

16 Know that a man is not justified by keeping God's laws, but by his faith in Jesus Christ. We are justified by our faith in Christ, and not by the works of the law, for by the works of the law shall no flesh be justified.

20 I am crucified with Christ; nevertheless, Christ lives in me, and the life which I now live in the flesh I live by my faith in the Son of God, who loved and gave himself for me.

21 I try not to disappoint God's grace, for if righteousness came by the law, then Christ died in vain.

Galatians 3

6 Even Abraham believed God, and it was accounted to him for righteousness.

8 The scriptures foresaw that God would justify the unbeliever through faith. They preached the gospel to Abraham, saying, In you shall all nations be blessed.

9 Those people of faith are blessed with faithful Abraham.

10 Many who are living by the law are under its curse, for it is written, Cursed is everyone who is not keeping all things which are written in the book of the law.

13 Christ has redeemed us from the curse of the law, being made a curse

for us, for it is written, Cursed is everyone who hangs on a tree. (Pointing to Christ and the cross.)

19 Do you keep the law? It was given to us because of sin until the seed should come to whom the promise was made, and it was ordained by angels in the hand of a mediator. (Christ)

22 The scripture is all about us being sinners, so that the promise by faith in Jesus Christ might be given to those who believe.

26 You are all children of God, only by faith in Christ Jesus.

29 If you are Christ's, then you are Abraham's seed and heirs according to that promise.

Galatians 4

5 Christ came to redeem those who were under the law, that we might receive God's adoption as sons.

6 Because you are sons, God has sent the Spirit of his Son into your hearts.

7 Now you are no longer a servant, but a son, and if a son, then an heir of God through Christ.

9 After you are known as God's, why turn again to the world and desire again to be tied to sin?

17 False teachers are eager to affect you; they deceive to exclude you in order to reach their goals.

Galatians 5

5 Through the Spirit we wait for the hope of righteousness by faith.

14 All of the law is fulfilled in one word, love. You shall love your neighbor as yourself.

16 Walk in the Spirit, and you shall not fulfil the lust of the flesh.

17 The flesh lusts against the Spirit and the Spirit against the flesh, so that you cannot do the things that you should.

22-23 The fruit of the Spirit is love, joy, peace, long-suffering, gentleness, goodness, faith, meekness, and self-control. Against those there is no law.

24 Those who are Christ's have crucified the flesh with its affections and lusts.

Galatians 6

3 If a man thinks himself to be something when he is nothing, he deceives himself.

4 Let every man prove his own work. Then shall he have rejoicing in himself alone and not in another.

7 Do not be deceived. God is not mocked, for whatever a man sows, that shall he also reap.

8 He who sows to his flesh shall of the flesh reap corruption, but he who sows to the Spirit shall of the Spirit reap life everlasting.

9 Let us not be weary in well doing, for in due season we shall reap if we faint not.

18 May the grace of our Lord Jesus Christ be with your spirit. Amen.

Ephesians

Adoption is mentioned a number of times in Scripture. It is important to understand what that means. Today, many people speak as if all children are God's children. This is not true. If it were, then they would be joint heirs with Christ, and Christ's death would be in vain. The Scriptures say we "become" children only by adoption. The meaning of adoption is unique to Christianity. We saw it in Galatians 4, and again we will find it here in Ephesians.

Ephesians 1

3 Blessed be the God and Father of our Lord Jesus Christ, who has blessed us with all spiritual blessings in heavenly places in Christ.

5 God predestinated us to be God's adopted children by Jesus Christ to himself, according to the good pleasure of his will.

7 In Jesus we have redemption through his blood and the forgiveness of sins according to the riches of his grace.

13-14 In Jesus you trusted. After that you heard the Word of truth, the gospel of your salvation. Then you believed and were sealed with the Holy Spirit, which is the assurance of our inheritance until the redemption of ourselves to the praise of his glory.

22 God has put all things under Christ's feet and made him to be the head over all things to the church.

23 The church is his body, the fullness of Christ, who fills all in all.

Ephesians 2

8-9 It is by grace that are you saved through faith, not by yourselves. It is the gift of God, not of works, so that no man can boast.

13 In Christ Jesus you who were sometimes far off are made near by the blood of Christ.

15 Christ abolished in his flesh the rebellion we have for his law of commandments, making Jews and Gentiles one people in Christ. He did

this by ending the system of law with its commandments and regulations.
He made peace between Jews and Gentiles by creating in himself one new
people from the two groups.
18 Through Christ, Jews and Gentiles have access by one Spirit to the Father.
20-21 We are built upon the foundation laid by the apostles and prophets,
with Jesus Christ himself being the chief corner stone in whom our body is
framed together, growing into a holy temple in the Lord.

Ephesians 3

7 I, Paul, was made a minister, according to the gift of the grace of God
given to me by the effective working of his power.
12 In Christ we have boldness and access to God with confidence by our
faith in Christ.
17 May Christ dwell in your hearts by faith, by being rooted and firm in love.
19 Know the love of Christ, which is beyond our comprehension, that you
might be filled with all the fullness of God.
20 Now to him who is able to do exceeding abundantly above all that we
ask or think, according to the Spirit's power that works in us.

Ephesians 4

2-3 Be patient, with all lowliness, meekness, and long suffering, bearing
up one another in love. Endeavour to keep the unity of the Spirit in the bond
of peace.
4 There is one body and one Spirit, even as you are called in one hope of
your calling.
5-6 There is one Lord, one faith, one baptism, one God and Father of us
all, who is above all, through all, and in all of us.
15 Speak the truth in love; mature in Christ in all things, who is our head.
17 I testify in the Lord that you need to walk not as other Gentiles walk.
They walk in their pride.
24 Put on your "new man," who is created in God's righteousness and true
holiness.
26 Be angry and sin not; let not the sun go down upon your wrath.
29 Let no corrupt words proceed out of your mouth, only that which is
edifying, that it may minister grace to the hearers.
30 Grieve not the Holy Spirit of God; reflect that you are sealed to the day
of redemption.
32 Be kind to one another, tenderhearted, forgiving one another, even as
God for Christ's purposes has forgiven you.

Ephesians 5

1 Be followers of God as his dear children.
2 Walk in love as Christ has loved and given himself for us, an offering and sacrifice to God.
3 Fornication, covetousness, and all uncleanness, let them not be once named among you saints.
4 Neither let filthiness, foolish talking, or jesting be named among you, but rather, keep giving thanks.
6 Let no man deceive you with worthless words; this causes the wrath of God to come upon the children of disobedience.
11 Have no fellowship with the fruitless works of darkness, but rather correct them.
15 See that you walk with integrity, not as fools, but as wise.
18 Do not be drunk with wine; that is excessive, but be filled with God's Spirit.
23 The husband is the head of the wife, even as Christ is the head of the church, and he is the Savior of the body.
24 Therefore, as the church is subject to Christ, so let the wives be subject to their own husbands in everything.
25-27 Husbands, love your wives, even as Christ loved the church and gave himself for it, that he might sanctify and cleanse it with the washing of water by the Word and present it to himself a glorious church, not having spot or wrinkle, or any such thing, but that it should be holy and without blemish.
31 For marriage shall a man leave his father and mother and be joined to his wife, and the two shall become one flesh.

Ephesians 6

1 Children, obey your parents in the Lord, for this is right.
3 So that it may be well with you, and you may live long on the earth.
4 You fathers, provoke not your children to wrath, but bring them up in the nurture and admonition of the Lord.
5 Servants, be obedient to your masters according to the flesh. Serve with fear and trembling, as to Christ.
8 Know that whatever a good man does, the same shall he receive of the Lord, whether he be a slave or free.
11 Put on the whole armor of God so that you may be able to stand against the temptations of the Devil.
18 Pray always, with all requests guided by the Holy Spirit.
24 Grace be with all who love our Lord Jesus Christ in sincerity. Amen.

Philippians

Are you reflecting Christ to the world? Desire to be an image of Christ to the world around you, as Paul did.

Philippians 1

2 Grace be to you and peace from God our Father and from the Lord Jesus Christ.
6 Being confident of this very thing, that he who has begun a good work in you will perform it until the day of Jesus Christ.
11 Be filled with the fruits of righteousness, which are by Jesus Christ, to the glory and praise of God.
20 According to my earnest expectation and hope, in nothing shall I be ashamed, but with all boldness Christ shall be magnified in my body, whether it be by life or by death.
27 Only let your conversations be a reflection of the gospel of Christ. Stand fast in one spirit and one mind, working together to further the faith of the gospel.
28 Never be terrified by your enemies; it is to them evidence of their evilness over you.

Philippians 2

3 Let nothing be done through anger or self-pride, but with a humble mind, allowing others to appear better than yourself.
4 Look not only after your own things, but also look after the things of others.
5 Let this mind be in you, which is also in Christ Jesus.
6-7 Christ, being in the form of God, thought it not robbery to be equal with God; he made himself of no reputation. He took upon himself the form of a servant and was made in the likeness of men.
10-11 At hearing the name of Jesus, every knee should bow: the things in heaven, on earth, and under the earth, and every tongue should confess that Jesus Christ is Lord, to the glory of God the Father.
12 My beloved, work out your own salvation with fear and trembling.
13 It is God who works in you, both to will and to do of his good pleasure.
14-15 Do all things without regret so that you may be blameless and harmless sons of God, without rebuke, in the midst of a crooked and perverse nation, among whom you shine as lights in the world.

Philippians 3

8 I count all things as nothing when compared to the excellent knowledge of Christ Jesus my Lord.
9 Be found in Christ, not having your own righteousness, which is of the law, but by that which is through faith in Christ, the righteousness which is of God by faith.
10-11 Know Christ, the power of his resurrection, and the fellowship of his sufferings, being made conformable to his death, that you may be resurrected from the dead.
14 I press toward the mark for the prize of the high calling of God in Christ Jesus.

Philippians 4

6 Be anxious for nothing, but in everything by prayer and supplication with thanksgiving let your requests be made known to God.
7 The peace of God, which passes all understanding, shall keep your hearts and minds safe through Christ Jesus.
8 Finally, brethren, whatever things are true, whatever things are honest, whatever things are just, whatever things are pure, whatever things are lovely, whatever things are good to report, if there be any goodness, and if there be any praise, think on these things.
13 I can do all things through Christ who strengthens me.
19 God will supply all your needs from his glorious riches, which have been given to us by Christ Jesus.

Colossians

Colossians is about making Christ your first focus in life. Your new life in Christ will bring glory to God, and you can become his light in your part of the world.

Colossians 1

13 God has delivered us from the power of darkness and has moved us into the kingdom of his dear Son.
15 Christ is the image of the invisible God, the firstborn of every creature.
18 Christ is the head of the body, the church. He is the beginning, the firstborn from the dead, that in all things he might have the superior place.
19 It pleased the Father that in Christ should all things be complete.

20 Having made peace through the blood of Christ's cross, God reconciled all things to himself, by Christ, whether they be things on earth, or things in heaven.

22 In Christ's flesh, through his death, Christ presents you holy, blameless, and sinless in his sight.

28 We preach Christ; we warn and teach every man, in all wisdom, that we may present him perfect in Christ Jesus.

Colossians 2

8 Beware, so no man fool you through philosophy and deceit after the traditions of men and the things of this world. Follow after Christ.

9 In Christ dwells all the fullness of the Godhead bodily.

12 Buried with Christ in baptism, you are raised with him through faith in God, who has raised Christ from the dead.

13 You were dead in your sins, but you have been made one with Christ. He has forgiven all your sins.

20 When you died with Christ, you may still live in the world, but you are not condemned by the law.

Colossians 3

1 When you are risen with Christ, seek those things which are heavenly, where Christ sits on the right hand of God.

4 When Christ, who is our life, shall appear, then shall you also appear with him in glory.

5 Take control of the way you live upon the earth. Fornication, uncleanness, inappropriate affection, evil desires, and covetousness are really idolatry.

10 Put on the "new man," who is renewed in knowledge after the image of Christ who created him.

11 There is neither Greek nor Jew, circumcision nor uncircumcision, Barbarian, Scythian, bond, nor free, but Christ is all and in all.

15 Let the peace of God rule in your hearts, to which you are called in one body, and be thankful.

16 Let the Word of Christ dwell in you richly in all wisdom and teaching. Encourage one another in psalms, hymns, and spiritual songs. Sing with grace in your heart to the Lord.

17 Whatever you do in word or deed, do all in the name of Jesus, giving thanks to God by him.

18 Wives, submit yourselves to your own husbands as it is right in the Lord.

19 Husbands, love your wives, and do not be bitter against them.

20 Children, obey your parents in all things, for this is well pleasing to the Lord.

21 Fathers, do not provoke your children to anger; they may become discouraged.

22 Servants, obey your masters according to the flesh in respect to God.

23 Whatever you do, do it heartily as to the Lord and not to men.

24 Know that you shall receive the Lord's reward of inheritance because you serve the Lord Jesus.

25 He who does wrong shall receive punishment. God does not show favor unjustly.

Colossians 4

5 Walk in wisdom with the unbeliever, redeeming the time. Let your speech be with grace, seasoned with salt, so that you may be thoughtful in how you ought to answer every man.

1 Thessalonians

These next two letters to the Thessalonian people challenge us to live for Christ. He is coming again for his own. Stand up and look expectantly for his coming. Share your faith in Christ with others.

1 Thessalonians 3

12 The Lord causes you to increase and abound in love one toward another and toward all men.

13 Christ will establish your hearts blameless, holy before God our Father when he comes with all his saints.

1 Thessalonians 4

1 We ask and encourage you, as representatives of the Lord Jesus. You have received from us how you ought to walk and please God, so that you can do more and more.

3 This is the will of God, even your sanctification, that you should abstain from fornication.

6 No man should defraud his brother in any matter because the Lord punishes all who do.

7 God has not called us to uncleanness, but to holiness.

8 He who despises another person despises God, who has given us his Holy Spirit.

11 Study to be quiet and to do your own business; work with your own hands as we command.

14 If we believe that Jesus died and rose again, God will bring those who sleep in Jesus with him.

15 By the Word of the Lord, we who are alive and remain at the coming of the Lord shall not prevent those who are asleep.

16-17 At his second coming, the Lord shall descend from heaven with a shout, with the voice of the archangel, and with the trump of God. The dead in Christ shall rise first; then, we who are alive shall be caught up together with them in the clouds to meet the Lord in the air, and we shall ever be with the Lord.

1 Thessalonians 5

2 You know perfectly that the Day of the Lord comes as a thief in the night.

6 Let us not sleep as others do, but let us watch and be sober.

8 Let us who are of the day be sober, putting on the breastplate of faith and love and the helmet of the hope of salvation.

9 God has not appointed us to receive his wrath, but to obtain salvation by our Lord Jesus Christ.

10 Christ died for us so that whether we live or die, we shall live together with him.

11 Comfort yourselves together and teach one another.

12 Know those who labor among you, those who are over you in the Lord, and those who discipline you.

13 Consider highly your leaders in the Lord with love, for their work's sake. And be at peace among yourselves.

14 We encourage you to warn those who are unruly, comfort the feebleminded, support the weak, and be patient toward all men.

15 See that no one uses evil against evil toward any man; follow that which is good, both among yourselves and to all men.

16-17 Rejoice evermore. Pray without ceasing.

18 In everything give thanks, for this is the will of God in Christ Jesus concerning you.

19 Quench not the Spirit.

20-21 Do not despise prophesying. Prove all things; hold fast to that which is good.

22 Avoid all appearance of evil.

23 May the very God of peace sanctify you wholly, and I pray to God that your whole spirit, soul, and body be preserved blameless to the coming of our Lord Jesus Christ.

28 The grace of our Lord Jesus Christ be with you. Amen.

2 Thessalonians 1

6 It is a righteous thing with God to act against the sin of those who trouble you.

7 You who are troubled, rest with us. Know that the Lord Jesus will come from heaven with his mighty angels.

9 Your enemy will be punished with everlasting destruction from the presence of the Lord and from the glory of his power.

2 Thessalonians 3

1 Finally, pray for us, that the Word of the Lord may go forward and the Lord is glorified.

3 The Lord is faithful; he shall establish you and keep you from evil.

5 The Lord directs your hearts into the love of God and into the patient waiting for Christ.

6 Now we command you, in the name of our Lord Jesus Christ, that you withdraw yourselves from every brother who walks disorderly.

10 This we commanded you, that if any capable person will not work, neither should they eat.

18 The grace of our Lord Jesus Christ be with you all. Amen.

1 Timothy

Paul wrote Timothy several letters. In these letters we reap wisdom. We are encouraged to be bold and not ashamed to share Christ with others because of what he has done for us as our Redeemer. Step out in faith and allow the Holy Spirit to live in and through your life. If you have not received Christ into your life, humble yourself and invite him in.

1 Timothy 1

2 Grace, mercy, and peace from God our Father and Jesus Christ our Lord.

5 The last commandment is that you love out of a pure heart, a good conscience, and genuine faith.

10-11 Sexually immoral people defile themselves with mankind. So also do homosexuals, liars, perjured persons, and those who violate the sound doctrine of the gospel.

15 This is a faithful saying: Christ Jesus came into the world to save sinners.
17 Now to the King eternal, immortal, invisible, the only wise God, be honor and glory forever and ever. Amen.
19 Hold to the faith and keep a good conscience.

1 Timothy 2

1 I instruct you that your requests, prayers, intercessions, and giving of thanks, be made for all men.
5 There is one God and one mediator between God and men, the man Christ Jesus.
8 I ask that men pray everywhere, lifting up holy hands without anger or doubting.
10 Women profess godliness with their good works.

1 Timothy 3

2-3 The overseer of the church must be above reproach, the husband of only one wife, temperate, self-controlled, respectable, hospitable, able to teach, not given to drunkenness, not violent, not quarrelsome, not a lover of money.
15 Know how you ought to behave in the house of God, which is the church, the pillar, and the ground for the truth.

2 Timothy

2 Timothy 1

2 Grace, mercy, and peace from God the Father and Jesus Christ our Lord.
7 God has not given us the spirit of fear, but of power, of love, and of a sound mind.
8 Do not be ashamed of our Lord, but share in suffering for the gospel, according to the power of God.
9 God has saved us and called us with a holy calling, not according to our works, but according to his own purpose and grace, which were given to us in Christ Jesus before the world began.
12 I suffered for the cause of these things; nevertheless, I am not ashamed, for I know whom I have believed and am persuaded that he is able to keep that which I have committed to him until that day of judgment.
14 The truth was given to us to keep by the Holy Spirit who dwells in us.

2 Timothy 2

10 I endure all things for the elect's sakes, that they may also obtain the salvation which is in Christ Jesus with eternal glory.

11-13 It is a faithful saying, For if we are dead with him, we shall also live with him. If we suffer, we shall also reign with him; if we deny him, he will also deny us. If we believe not, yet he remains faithful, for he cannot deny himself.

15 Study to show yourself approved to God, a workman who does not need to be ashamed, rightly and carefully studying the Word of truth.

16 Avoid profane and worthless talk, for it will lead to more ungodliness.

19 The foundation of God stands sure; the Lord knows those who are his. Let everyone who names the name of Christ depart from sin.

22 Flee youthful lusts. Follow righteousness, faith, love, and peace. Join with those who call on the Lord out of a pure heart.

23 Avoid foolish and unlearned questions; know that they cause disagreements.

24-25 The servant of the Lord must not be self-important, but must be gentle to all men, able to teach, patient, and meek, while instructing those who oppose them. God's intervention may result in repentance so that they acknowledge the truth.

2 Timothy 3

1 This you should know; in the last days perilous times shall come.

12 Yes, and all who will live godly in Christ Jesus shall suffer persecution.

13 But evil men and seducers shall get worse and worse, deceiving and being deceived.

16 All scripture is given by inspiration of God and is profitable for doctrine, for debating, for correction, and for instruction in righteousness.

Titus

Paul's letter to Titus encourages us how to live. It also instructs us to teach truth. Truth must be the foundation of Christianity; otherwise, it is evil.

Titus 1

2-3 We have hope of eternal life, by God, who cannot lie, who promised it before the world began by the commandment of God our Savior.

4 Grace, mercy, and peace from God the Father and the Lord Jesus Christ, our Savior.

15 To those who are pure all things are pure, but to those who are defiled and unbelieving, nothing is pure; even their mind and conscience are defiled.

Titus 2

2 Aged men should be sober, self-controlled, sound in faith, charity, and patience.
3 Aged women should behave with holiness, not be false accusers, nor consumers of much wine, but they should be teachers of good things.
4-5 Older women are to teach the young women to be sober, to love their husbands, and to love their children. They are to be discreet, chaste, homemakers, good and obedient to their husbands, so that the Word of God is not blasphemed.
8 Speak the truth that cannot be condemned, so your opposer may be ashamed, having no evil thing to say about you.
11 The grace of God that brings salvation has appeared to all men.
12 Teach us to deny ungodliness and worldly lusts. We should live soberly, righteously, and godly in this present world.

Titus 3

1 Be subject to governments and authorities, obey the courts, and be ready to do good work.
2 Do not speak evil to any man, or fight, but be gentle and meek to all.
4-6 The kindness and love of God, our Savior, toward man appeared, not by works of righteousness which we have done, but according to his mercy. He saved us by the washing of regeneration and renewing of the Holy Spirit, which he shed on us abundantly through Jesus Christ, our Savior.
7 We are justified by his grace, that we should be made heirs according to the hope of eternal life.
9 Avoid foolish questions, genealogies, arguments, and differences about the law, for they are unprofitable.
10 After correcting a man twice, reject the man who is a heretic.

Philemon

Philemon is a short letter from Paul. He encourages us to give of ourselves out of our gratitude for our faith in Christ.

Philemon 1

3 Grace to you and peace from God our Father and the Lord Jesus Christ.
6 May witnessing to your faith become effective, by acknowledging every good thing which is in you in Christ Jesus.
25 The grace of our Lord Jesus Christ be with your spirit. Amen.

Hebrews

The book of Hebrews is about the supremacy of Christ. He alone satisfied God's judgment of death to pay for our sins, no matter how large or small.

In the complete book of the *Bible* you find many examples of "better" or "better than", which reflect the significance that Christ makes for us. We can never keep the law of the Ten Commandments, which are found in the OLD TESTAMENT, but Christ did.

Notice the word "perfect" or forms of that word. These words are used when describing Christ. Perfect means that it cannot be improved upon, or it would only be a comparative. If it is perfect, we can say it is truth. Christ said, "I am the way, the truth and the life." How enlightening that is. Truth and true are at the very top of any comparison, and that is where Christ dwells. If Christ is not comparable, Christ has to be God. If Christ were less than God, he would not be a perfect redeemer for sin and thus not holy enough. There is only one that is holy, and that is God. The same has to be true of the Holy Spirit. We read that Jesus is our Emmanuel, which means God with us. Now you have the doctrine of the Trinity, three in one.

There is nothing remotely equal to Christ, Christianity, or the *Bible*. This is inspiring. When you read all the other religion books in the world, nothing can compare, and Hebrews confirms that conclusion.

Hebrews 1

2 God has spoken to us by his Son, whom he has appointed heir of all things, by whom also he made the worlds.
3 Christ is the brightness of God's glory and the express image of his person, upholding all things by the power of his Word. When he had by himself purged our sins, he sat down on the right hand of the Majesty on high.
4 Christ was made so much better than the angels; he has by inheritance obtained a more excellent name than they.

8 God says to his Son, Your throne, oh God, is forever and ever, a scepter of righteousness is the scepter of your kingdom.

9 Christ, you have loved righteousness and hated sin; therefore, God has anointed you with the oil of gladness above all.

10-12 You, Lord, in the beginning have laid the foundation of the earth, and the heavens are the works of your hands. They shall perish, but you remain, and they all shall rot like old cloth.

14 All angels are ministering spirits sent forth to minister to those who shall be heirs of salvation.

Hebrews 2

2 The words spoken by angels are steadfast, and every transgression and disobedience receives a just punishment.

6-8 What is man that you are mindful of him, or the son of man that you visit him? You made man a little lower than the angels; you crowned him with glory and honor and set him over the works of your hands; you have put all things in subjection to him.

9 We see Jesus, who was made a little lower than the angels by suffering death. He was crowned with glory and honor that he, by the grace of God, should taste death for every man.

14 As much as God's children are partakers of flesh and blood, Christ also took part of the same, that through death he might destroy the Devil, who has the power of death.

Hebrews 3

4 Every house we see is built by some man, but he who built all things is God.

12 Take care that none of you has an evil heart of unbelief that would cause you to depart from the living God.

13 Warn one another daily: Take care so that none of you change your beliefs by the sin of deceit.

14 We are made partakers of Christ if we hold our faith in him firm to the end.

Hebrews 4

3 We who have believed enter into his rest, whose works were finished from the foundation of the world.

12 The Word of God is quick, powerful, and sharper than any two-edged sword; it pierces and divides the soul and spirit, and it discerns the thoughts and intents of the heart.

13 There is no creature that is not fully known in God's sight; all things are naked and open to his eyes.

14-16 We have a great high priest who passed into the heavens, Jesus the Son of God. Let us hold fast to our profession of faith. We have a high priest who feels our trials; he was in all points tempted like as we are, yet without sin. Let us come boldly to his throne of grace, that we may obtain mercy and find grace in our time of need.

Hebrews 5

4 No man takes the honor of offering sacrifices for sin to himself, but he who is called of God.

12 You ought to be teachers, but you still need someone to teach you again the first principles of the words of God; you are like a baby still needing milk and not mature enough to eat meat.

Hebrews 6

10 God is not unrighteous; he does not forget your work and labor of love, which you have shown toward his name by ministering to the saints.

15 After Abraham had patiently endured forty years in the wilderness, he obtained God's promise.

17 God was more than willing to show to the heirs of Abraham the immutability (unchanging) of his counsel. He confirmed it by his oath, before hand.

18 It is impossible for God to lie by two immutable things, his oath and his promise. We know that he is our refuge for the hope that is set before us.

Hebrews 7

16 Jesus is made, not after the law of a man-made commandment, but after the power of an endless life.

24-25 Jesus, who lives forever, has an unchangeable priesthood. He is able to save us to the ultimate by making intercession for us.

26 Christ our high priest became man. He is holy, harmless, undefiled, separate from sinners, and higher than the heavens.

Hebrews 8

6 Christ obtained a more excellent ministry. He is the mediator of a better covenant, which was established upon perfect promises.

Hebrews 9

12 It was not by the blood of goats and calves, but by his own blood that Christ was able to enter into the temple's Holy of Holies and obtain eternal redemption for us, once and for all.

15 Christ is the mediator of the NEW TESTAMENT, that by his death for the redemption of sins who were under that FIRST TESTAMENT, those who are called might receive the promise of eternal life.

22 Almost all things under the law are purged by blood. Without the shedding of blood there is no forgiveness of sin.

24 Christ did not enter into the holy places made by man, which represent heaven, but into heaven itself to appear before God for us.

25-26 Christ did not need to offer himself often as the people's priest offers sacrifices. For he is the perfect sacrifice since the foundation of the world and to the end of the world.

27-28 It is appointed to men once to die, but after this the judgment. So Christ was once offered to bear the sins of many. Those who look for him shall appear a second time without sin, having obtained salvation.

Hebrews 10

20-22 Christ, a new and living way, has consecrated us through the veil, his flesh. He is our high priest over the house of God. Let us then come near to God with a true heart in full assurance of faith because our hearts have been sprinkled clean from an evil conscience and our bodies washed with pure water.

29 How painful will the punishment be for those who have placed under their foot the Son of God, who declare the blood of Christ, by which man is sanctified, as an unholy thing and have rejected the Holy Spirit of grace?

31 As an offender of Christ, it is a fearful thing to fall into the hands of the living God.

Hebrews 11

1 Now faith is the substance of things hoped for, the evidence of things not seen.

3 Through faith we understand that the worlds were framed by the Word of God. Things which are seen were not made from things which already existed.

6 Without faith it is impossible to please God, for he who comes to God must believe that he is and that he is the rewarder of those who diligently seek him.

Hebrews 12

1-2 We are surrounded by a great cloud of witnesses. Let us put aside every sin which so easily trouble us, and let us run with patience the race that is set before us. Look to Jesus, the author and finisher of our faith, who for the joy that was set before him endured the cross, despising the shame and is seated at the right hand of the throne of God.

5 Despise not the discipline of the Lord nor faint when you are rebuked by him.

6 Those whom the Lord loves, he disciplines.

8 If you say you need no discipline, then you are illegitimate sons.

10 Our earthly fathers disciplined us after their own pleasure, but Christ does it for our profit, that we might be partakers of his holiness.

14 Live in peace with all men, with holiness, so men may see the Lord.

28 We received a kingdom which cannot be moved; let us have grace so that we may serve God acceptably, with reverence and godly fear.

Hebrews 13

4 Marriage is honorable, and the bed should be theirs alone, so sex outside of marriage and adulterers will be judged by God.

5 Let your conversation be without coveting. Be content with what you have. God has said, I will never leave you nor forsake you.

8 Jesus Christ is the same yesterday, today, and forever.

14 On earth we have no eternal city, but we seek one to come, the new Jerusalem.

20-21 May the God of peace, who brought Jesus from the dead, and who is the great shepherd of the sheep, through the blood of the everlasting covenant, make you perfect in every good work to do his will and to work in you that which is well pleasing in his sight through Jesus Christ, to whom be glory forever and ever. Amen.

James

The book of James is written as practical life applications. It is about faith and works. There are people who have taken James' verses out of context and attempted to put people under the law of good works. By doing so, they actually reject being saved by faith alone. A careful reading shows Christ's work on the cross is all sufficient and that works are an end product of our faith and love.

James 1

2 Count it all joy when you fall into various temptations.

3 Know this, that the trying of your faith works patience.

4 Let patience have its perfect work, that you may be perfect and complete, wanting nothing.

5 If any man lack wisdom, let him ask of God, who gives to all men liberally and scolds not. It shall be given him.

12 Blessed is the man who endures temptation, for when he is tried, he shall receive the crown of life, which the Lord has promised to those who love him.

13 Let no man say when he is tempted, I am tempted of God, for God cannot be tempted with evil; neither does he tempt any man.

14 Every man is tempted when he is drawn away by his own lust.

19 Let every man be swift to hear, slow to speak, and slow to get angry.

21 Lay aside all filthiness and evil. Receive with meekness God's written Word, which is able to save your souls.

22 Be doers of God's Word and not hearers only; do not deceive yourself.

26 If any man among you seems to be religious and does not control his tongue, he deceives his own heart and his religion is worthless.

James 2

5 God has chosen the poor of this world to be rich in faith and heirs of his kingdom, which he has promised to those who love him.

13 God shall have judgment without mercy on those who have shown no mercy.

17 Faith, if it is not combined by works, is dead. Faith and works stand together.

19 There is one God who is wise. The devils also believe and tremble.

20 Faith without works is dead.

24 It is by works that a man is justified and not by faith only.

James 3

1 Those who rule over others shall receive greater condemnation.

2 If any man does not offend by his words, the same is a perfect man and is able to control his whole body.

8-10 The tongue cannot be tamed; it is an unruly evil, full of deadly poison. This should not happen. We should not bless God and curse men out of the same mouth.

14-15 If you are bitter with envy and self-seeking in your hearts, do not boast and lie. This wisdom descends not from above, but is earthly and devilish.

18 The fruit of righteousness is sown in peace by those who make peace.

James 4

4 About adultery and this world, know that the friendship of the world is hostile against God.

6 Christ gives more grace. He resists the proud, but gives grace to the humble.

7 Submit yourselves to God. Resist the Devil, and he will flee from you.

8 Draw close to God, and he will draw close to you. Cleanse your hands and purify your hearts.

10 Humble yourselves in the sight of the Lord, and he shall lift you up.

14-15 You do not know what will happen tomorrow. Your life is for just a little time, so do not say what you will do tomorrow. You ought to say, If the Lord wills it, we shall live and do this or that.

17 He who knows to do good and does not do it, to him it is sin.

James 5

7 Be patient for the second coming of the Lord.

9 Grudge not one against another; take care that you are not condemned. Notice, the Judge stands in the doorway.

12 Above all things, swear not by heaven nor by the earth, neither by any other oath, but let your yes be yes and your no be no, so that you are not condemned.

15 The prayer of faith shall save the sick, and the Lord shall raise him up. If he has committed sins, they shall be forgiven him.

16 Confess your faults to one another, and pray for one another so that you may be healed. The effectual fervent prayer of a righteous man benefits much.

1 Peter

This book of 1st Peter says that your faith is far more precious than gold. Know that fact. Your faith will lift you above the pitfalls of human thinking. Once you are born again, you cannot lose the gift that God has guaranteed. Know who you are in Christ. Due to God's promise, your position is irrevocable. Live as Christ's ambassador.

1 Peter 1

3 Blessed be the God and Father of our Lord Jesus Christ, who according to his abundant mercy has born us again to a lively hope by the resurrection of Jesus Christ from the dead.

4 There is an incorruptible inheritance that is undefiled and fades not away reserved in heaven for you.

5 We are kept by the power of God through faith to salvation, ready to be revealed in the last days.

7 The trial of your faith is much more precious than gold tried with fire, so that it might be found to give praise, honor, and glory at the appearing of Jesus Christ.

9 The end of your faith results in the salvation of your soul.

13 Guard your mind, be sober, and hope to the end for the grace that will be brought to you at the revelation of Jesus Christ.

15 He who has called you is holy, so be holy in all manner of conversation.

20 God determined before the creation of the world to reveal Christ in these times to you.

21 Believe in God, who raised Christ up from the dead and gave him glory, that your faith and hope might be in God.

22 You have purified your souls in obeying the truth through the Spirit. See that you really love one another with a pure heart.

23 Being born again, not of corruptible seed, but of incorruptible, by the Word of God, which lives and abides forever.

24 All flesh is like grass, and all the glory of man is like the flower produced by that grass. The grass dies, and its flower falls away.

25 The Word of the Lord endures forever. This Word is the good news that is preached to you.

1 Peter 2

1 Lay aside all malice, guile, hypocrisies, envies, and evil speaking.

2 As newborn babes, desire the sincere milk of the Word that you may grow.

4 Christ is coming, as to a living stone, rejected by men, but chosen by God and precious.

5 We also as living stones, became a spiritual house, a holy priesthood, to offer up spiritual sacrifices acceptable to God by Jesus Christ.

7-8 To you believers, Christ is precious, but to those who are disobedient, the stone which the builders rejected, the same stone is made the head corner stone, a stumbling stone, and a rock of offense, even to those who stumble at the Word.

9 You are a chosen generation, a royal priesthood, a holy nation, a peculiar people. You should show forth the praises of Christ who has called you out of darkness into his marvellous light

10 In the past we were not a people, but now we are the people of God. We had not obtained mercy, but now we have.

11 As strangers and pilgrims, abstain from fleshly lusts, which war against the soul.

13 Submit yourselves to every ordinance of man for the Lord's purposes.

16 You are free, so do not use your liberty to cover maliciousness. Be as the servants of God.

21 We were called because Christ suffered for us, leaving us an example that we should follow his steps.

24 Christ received our sins in his own body on the cross, that we, being dead to sins, should live to righteousness, by whose stripes you were healed.

1 Peter 3

1-2 Wives, be in subjection to your husband, so that if they do not live by the Word, your clean conversations and fear may win them to the Word.

3-6 Let not your grooming find its importance in primping the hair, wearing jewelry, or fancy clothes, but let what is important be what is hidden in your heart.

7 Likewise, you husbands, live with your wife according to knowledge, giving honor to her, as to the weaker vessel and as being heirs together of the grace of life, so that your prayers will not be hindered.

9 Do not return evil for evil, but be a blessing; know that you are called, and that you shall inherit a blessing.

10 He who loves life and sees good days, let him stop his tongue from evil.

11 Turn from evil, and do good; seek peace, and participate in it.

12 The eyes of the Lord are over the righteous, and his ears are open to their prayers, but the face of the Lord is against those who do evil.

15 Sanctify the Lord God in your hearts, and be ready always to give an answer, with meekness and fear, to every man who asks you about the reason for the hope that is in you.

18 Christ has once suffered for sins, the just for the unjust, that he might bring us to God, being put to death in the flesh but raised up by the Spirit.

22 Christ has gone to heaven and is seated at the right hand of God; angels, authorities, and powers are subject to him.

1 Peter 4

1 As Christ has suffered for us in the flesh, arm yourselves likewise with

the same mind, for he who has suffered in the flesh has ceased from sin.

5 You shall give account to Christ who is ready to judge the quick and the dead.

7 The end of all things is at hand; be calm and go to prayer.

8 Above all things, share among yourselves, for your giving shall cover a multitude of sins.

9 Be hospitable one to another without complaining.

10 As every man has received the gift, minister the same one to another as good stewards of the grace of God.

14 If you are criticized for following Christ, be happy, for the spirit of glory and of God rests upon you.

16-17 If any man suffers for being a Christian, let him not be ashamed, but let him glorify God because of it. For the time has come when judgment must begin in the house of God. If it first begins with us, what shall be the end of those who disobey the gospel of God?

18 If the righteous are scarcely saved, where shall the ungodly and the sinner appear?

1 Peter 5

2 Teach the flock of God which is among you. Be a willing leader, but not for excessive reward.

4 When the chief Shepherd shall appear, you shall receive a crown of glory that does not fade away.

5 The young are to submit to their elders. All of you need to be subject one to another, so be humble, for God resists the proud and gives grace to the humble.

7 Throw all your care upon Christ, for he cares for you.

8 Be sober and vigilant because your critic the Devil goes around like a roaring lion, seeking those whom he may devour.

2 Peter

Peter encourages Christians to live their faith in the sight of non-believers. Our faith is not in vain. Christ is our Lord and Savior. Be proud to be called a Christian because you are a child of God. If you're not a Christian already, consider the Spirit's call on your life and respond to God's love.

2 Peter 1

2 Grace and peace be multiplied to you through the knowledge of God and of Jesus our Lord.

3 God's divine power has given us all things that pertain to life and godliness.

4 He has given us exceeding great and precious promises, that by these you might be partakers of the divine nature, having escaped the corruption that is in the world through lust.

10 Be aware to make your calling and election sure, for if you do these things, you shall never fall.

16 We have not followed clever made up stories when we made known to you the power and coming of our Lord Jesus Christ, but we were eyewitnesses of his majesty.

17 Christ received from God honor and glory when a voice came to earth from heaven saying, This is my beloved Son, in whom I am well pleased.

20 Know this first; no prophecy of the scripture is of any private interpretation.

2 Peter 2

12 False teachers speak evil of the things they do not understand and shall completely perish in their own corruption.

19-21 False teachers promise liberty, but they themselves are the servants of corruption. By them a man is overcome and brought into bondage.

2 Peter 3

10 The Day of the Lord will come as a thief in the night; the heavens shall pass away with a great noise, and the elements shall melt with fervent heat. The earth also and the works that are here shall be burned up.

15 The long suffering of our Lord is salvation, even as Paul wrote according to the wisdom given to him.

17 You have known these things, so do not be led away by the errors of the wicked.

18 Grow in grace and in the knowledge of our Lord and Savior Jesus Christ. To him be glory, both now and forever. Amen.

1 John

The book of 1st John addresses man's sin issue. Christ is our advocate with the Father. Sin is breaking the laws and instructions that God has set forth. But, because God is pure love, we have Christ. He is willing to save us from the penalty for sin by placing our sin upon himself.

1 John 5:20 tells us that Christ is God. Therefore, he is our perfect redeemer before a perfectly holy God.

1 John 1

5 This then is the message which we have heard of Christ and declare to you: God is light, and in him is no darkness at all.

7 If we walk in the light, as he is in the light, we have fellowship one with another, and the blood of Jesus Christ his Son cleanses us from all sin.

8 If we say that we have no sin, we deceive ourselves, and the truth is not in us.

9 If we confess our sins, he is faithful and just to forgive us our sins and to cleanse us from all unrighteousness.

1 John 2

1 My little children, these things I write to you, that you sin not. And if any man sins, we have an advocate with the Father, Jesus Christ the righteous.

4 He who says, I know Christ and keeps not his commandments is a liar, and the truth is not in him.

6 He who says he abides in Christ ought to walk even as he walked.

11 He who hates his brother is in darkness and walks in darkness. He knows not where he goes because that darkness has blinded his eyes.

17 The world passes away, and so does lust, but he who does the will of God abides forever.

18 Little children, it is the last days. You have heard that the Antichrist shall come, but even now there are many antichrists, so we know that it is the last days.

22 Who is a liar? He who denies that Jesus is the Christ. He is antichrist, who denies the Father and the Son.

23 Whoever denies the Son, the same has not the Father; he who acknowledges the Son has the Father also.

24 Let the Son abide in you, which you have heard from the beginning. If what you heard from the beginning shall remain in you, you shall continue in the Son and in the Father.

27 The anointing you have received from Christ abides in you. You need no teachers because the anointing of the Holy Spirit teaches you all things. It is the truth, you shall abide in Christ.

28 Now, little children, abide in Christ, so when he shall appear, we may have confidence and not be ashamed before him at his coming.

1 John 3

4 Whoever commits sin breaks the law. Sin is the breaking of God's law.

5 You know that Christ came to take away our sins, and in him is no sin.

9 Whoever is born of God should not continue in a lifestyle of sin, for Christ's seed resides in him. He cannot sin onto death because he is born of God.

11 This is the message that you heard from the beginning: We should love one another.

13 Marvel not if the world hates you.

15 Whoever hates his brother is a murderer, and you know that no murderer has eternal life abiding in himself.

17 Whoever has this world's goods, sees his brother in need, and withholds his compassion from him, how does the love of God dwell in him?

20 If our heart condemns us, God is greater than our heart and knows all things.

23 This is God's commandment: Believe on the name of his Son Jesus Christ and love one another.

1 John 4

3 Every spirit that does not confess that Jesus Christ has come in the flesh is not of God, and this is the spirit of antichrist. You have heard that he would come and even now is in the world.

8 He who does not love God does not know God, for God is love.

10 This is love, not that we loved God, but that he loved us and sent his Son to be the propitiation (atonement) for our sins.

15 Whoever shall confess that Jesus is the Son of God, God dwells in him and he in God.

18 There is no fear in love, but perfect love throws out fear because fear is torment. He who has fear is not made perfect in love.

1 John 5

1 Whoever believes that Jesus is the Christ is born of God, and everyone who loves God loves Christ.

3 This is the love of God, that we keep his commandments, and his commandments are not grievous.

6 This is he who came by water and blood, Jesus Christ, not by water only, but by water and blood. It is the Spirit who bears witness because the Spirit is truth.

7-8 There are three who bear record in heaven: the Father, the Word, and the Holy Ghost; these three are one. And there are three who bear witness on earth: the Spirit, the water, and the blood; these three agree in one.

12 He who has the Son has life; he who has not the Son of God has not life.

18 We know that whoever is born of God sins not onto death, but he who is begotten by God keeps himself, and the wicked one touches him not.

20 We know that the Son of God has come and has given us an under
standing, that we may know him who is true, and we are in him who is true;
we are in his Son Jesus Christ. This is the true God and eternal life.
21 Little children, keep yourselves from idols. Amen.

2 John

This second book written by John may be short, but it warns us clearly that
there are people and religions who deny the truths about God, even some
so-called Christian churches. You can identify them by their teachings.
They pick and choose what they want to believe for their own comfort.
They reject some of the disciples' and apostles' teaching in the *Bible*. Luke
11:35 warns us to "Make sure that the light we are following is not really
darkness." God inspired the writings in the *Bible,* and there are no doctrinal
untruths in it. So, rightly divide the Word and study it to show yourself
approved in doing so.

2 John 1

6 This is love, that we walk after God's commandments.
9 Whoever sins and abides not in the doctrine of Christ has not God. He
who abides in the doctrine of Christ, has both the Father and the Son.
10 If anyone comes to you and does not bring this doctrine, do not receive
him into your house; neither bid him God's speed.

3 John

The book of 3rd John admonishes us to walk in the truth and to support
fellow Christians who travel through our community. We are to be
hospitable to those who share the true faith that is in Christ Jesus.

3 John 1

4 I have no greater joy than to hear that my children walk in truth.
5 Be faithful. Whatever you do for the local brethren, do also for fellow
believers who may be strangers traveling through.
11 Do not follow evil; follow that which is good. He who does good is of
God, but he who does evil has not seen God.

Jude

In these last days before Christ returns, there are those who are fighting against the church. The fight is basically about truth. Truth that is compromised is not truth. Truth is an absolute. John encourages us to build up our brothers and sisters in the faith. We are to teach sound doctrine, so that we do not fall for lies that non-Christian religions put before us.

Jude 1

18-19 You were told there would be mockers who will walk after their own ungodly lusts in the last days. These people separate themselves from believers and are sensual, not having the Spirit.

20 Build up your most holy faith, praying in the Holy Spirit.

21 Keep yourselves in the love of God, looking for the mercy of our Lord Jesus Christ, which results in eternal life.

22-23 Some of you have compassion and make a big difference witnessing. Others save some people with fear, pulling them out of the eternal fire.

24-25 Now to him who is able to keep you from falling and to present you faultless before the presence of God's glory with exceeding joy, to the only wise God our Savior, be glory and majesty, dominion and power, both now and forever. Amen.

Revelation

Revelation, written by John, is the last book in the *Holy Bible*. It covers past, present and future history, but centers on Christ's second coming to earth. Study and research help us in our understanding. Many of the meanings within its words are spiritually discerned, which test the heart. Study this book with a group of people and use a *Bible* commentary to give yourself more understanding. This book is mainly about a seven year period known as the Tribulation period followed by a thousand year Millennium period.

On the very first day of the Tribulation, Christians will be caught-up in the air to be with Christ. Then, during the first three and a half years, the world's people accept a world leader to rule over them. This leader offers a false peace and issues a world personal identity system known in the book of Revelation as the Mark of the Beast, whose identity is also known as the

151

number 666. The people who accept this identity have a false hope when the author of this system, Satan, takes control.

During the second three and a half years God will strike the world with disaster and judgment, followed by Satan being bound captive and Christ coming back to earth with his Saints to reign a thousand years in righteousness.

After the thousand years, Satan will be released to make a final war against Christ before he is defeated and thrown into everlasting Hell, along with all those who reject Christ's dominion.

The ending chapters describe in beautiful detail what awaits all those who have made a decision to trust in Christ and put their faith in the truths of God's Word. We who have accepted Christ as our personal Savior will affirm that our faith was not in vain, and that Christ's promises were all true. This earth will then pass away, and Heaven will be our eternal reward for our faith in Christ.

The book of Revelation can be trusted. It is based upon the foundation of truth that has been meticulously maintained in the *Bible,* from cover to cover.

Revelation 1

3 Blessed is the person who reads, hears, and keeps the words of this prophecy which are written here, for the end time is approaching.
5 It is Jesus Christ who loved us and washed us from our sins with his own blood.
7 When Christ returns, he will come out of the clouds, and every eye shall see him, including those who crucified him. All people of the earth shall wail because of him. Even so, Amen.
8 The Lord said, I am the Alpha and Omega, the beginning and the end, who is, and who was, and who is to come, the Almighty.
18 I am he who now lives and was dead. Behold, I am alive forevermore. Amen. I have the keys to Hell and death.

Revelation 2

7 He that has an ear, let him hear what the Spirit says.
25 Of that which you have already, hold fast until I come.

Revelation 3

5 Christ said, He that overcomes, the same shall be clothed in white, and I

will not blot his name from of the book of life, but I will confess his name before my Father and before his angels.

11 Behold, I come quickly; hold fast to that which you have, so no man can take your crown.

15 I know what you do; you are neither hot nor cold toward me.

16 Because you are lukewarm, I will spit you out of my mouth.

19 As many as I love, I rebuke and correct; be zealous to repent.

20 Notice, I stand at the door and knock. If any man hears my voice and opens the door, I will come to him and will eat with him and he with me.

Revelation 4   (The Tribulation Period - 7 years long)

1 A door was opened in Heaven, and an angel's voice said, John, come up here, and I will show you what must take place.

2-3 Before me was a throne in Heaven with someone sitting on it who had the appearance of a jasper and sardine stone.

4 Surrounding the throne were twenty-four other thrones occupied by twenty-four elders.

5 There were seven lamps of fire burning before the throne, which were the seven Spirits of God.

6 In front of God's throne was a sea of glass like crystal, and in the middle and round the throne were four beasts full of eyes.

8 The four beasts had six wings and did not rest day or night, saying, Holy, holy, holy, LORD God Almighty, who was, and is, and is to come.

Revelation 5

1 I, John, saw in the right hand of him who sat on the throne a book that was sealed with seven seals.

2 I saw a strong angel proclaiming, Who is worthy to open the book and to loose the seals?

3 No man in Heaven or on earth was able to open the book.

5 One of the elders in Heaven said to me, Weep not, the Lion of the tribe of Judah, the Root of David, who is Christ is able to open the book and to release its seven seals of judgment.

9 The elders in Heaven sang a new song, You are worthy to open its seals.

12 The heavenly beings said with a loud voice, Worthy is the Lamb who was slain. He has received power, wisdom, strength, honor, and blessings.

14 The four beasts said, Amen, and the twenty-four elders worshiped him.

Revelation 6

1-2 When the Lamb, Christ, opened the first seal, it revealed a white horse, whose rider had a bow. He went forth to conquer.

3-4 The second seal revealed a red horse, whose rider took peace from the earth.

5-6 The third seal revealed a black horse, whose rider had a pair of balances in his hand to measure out wheat for a penny.

7-8 The fourth seal revealed a pale horse, whose rider was Death, and Hell followed with him.

9-11 The fifth seal revealed, under an altar, the souls of those who were slain for the Word of God and for the testimony which they held. They cried with a loud voice, saying, How long, oh Lord, holy and true, do you not judge and avenge our blood? Then white robes were given to them all.

12 The sixth seal revealed a great earthquake. The sun became black, the moon became as blood, and the stars of heaven fell to the earth.

15-17 All the great and powerful men on earth hid themselves in caves and under rocks of the mountains and said, Fall on us; hide us from the face of him who sits on the throne and from the wrath of the Lamb which is to come.

Revelation 7

3 An angel said, Do not harm the land or the sea or the trees until a seal is put on the foreheads of the servants of our God. I heard the number of those who were sealed. It was 144,000, representing all twelve tribes of Israel.

9 After this I saw a great multitude of people in Heaven, which no man could number, of all nations and tongues. Clothed with white robes and waving palm branches, they stood before the throne and before the Lamb.

10 All the angels cried with a loud voice, Salvation to our God who sits upon the throne and to the Lamb.

12 Blessings, glory, wisdom, thanksgiving, honor, power, and might be to our God forever and ever. Amen.

13-14 One of the elders said to me, Who are these who are arrayed in white robes, and where did they come from? I replied, Sir, you know. Then he said to me, These are those who came out of great tribulation and washed their robes white in the blood of the Lamb.

16 They shall neither hunger or thirst any more; neither shall the sun shine on them nor will they suffer from the heat.

17 The Lamb shall feed his followers and lead them to living fountains of waters, and God shall wipe away all their tears from their eyes.

Revelation 8

1 When Christ opened the seventh and last seal, there was silence in Heaven for about half an hour.

2 The seven angels who stand before God were given seven trumpets.

7 The first angel sounded his trumpet, and there came hail and fire mixed with blood, which was hurled down upon the earth. A third of the earth and a third of the trees were burned up, and all the green grass was burned up.

8-9 The second angel sounded his trumpet, and something like a huge mountain, all ablaze, was thrown into the sea. A third of the sea turned into blood, a third of the sea creatures died, and a third of the ships were destroyed.

10-11 The third angel sounded his trumpet, and a great star fell onto a third of the rivers and springs of water. A third of the waters turned bitter, killing many people.

12 The fourth angel sounded his trumpet, and a third of the sun, moon, and stars were struck.

13 As I watched, I heard an eagle call out in a loud voice: Woe! Woe! Woe to the inhabitants of the earth because of the trumpet blasts about to be sounded by the other three angels.

Revelation 9

1-2, 6 The fifth angel sounded his trumpet, which revealed the bottomless pit from where great smoke arose. In those days men shall seek death and shall not find it.

14-15, 18, 21 The sixth angel sounded his trumpet, saying, Loose the four angels which are bound in the great Euphrates River so they may slay the third part of men by the fire, smoke, and brimstone. Those who remained would not repent of their evil deeds.

Revelation 10

1-2 I saw another mighty angel come down from Heaven. He had in his hand a little book that was open.

5-6 The angel lifted up his hand toward Heaven and swore by him who lives forever and ever that time should be no longer.

7-9 The seventh angel sounded his trumpet, so that the mystery of God should be finished. And the voice said, Go and take the little book which is open in the hand of the angel. Take and eat the little book. It shall make your belly bitter, but in your mouth it shall be as sweet as honey.

10-11 So I took the little book and ate it. Then he said to me, You must prophesy again before many people, nations, tongues, and kings.

Revelation 11

1-2 I, John, was told to measure the temple of God and its altar and count those who worshiped there, but I was to leave the outer court out, for it was given to the Gentiles who would tread Jerusalem under foot forty-two months.

3, 5 Christ gave power to his two witnesses clothed in sackcloth to prophesy 1260 days. If any man hurt them, they were to be killed.

6 These two witnesses had the power to stop it from raining for all those days and to strike the earth with all plagues as often as they wanted.

7-10 When they finished their testimony, Satan made war against them and killed them. Their dead bodies lay in the street of the great city where Christ was crucified. And the world saw their dead bodies three and a half days. There people rejoiced over them.

11 After the three and a half days, the spirit of life from God entered into them. When they stood up great fear fell upon those who saw them.

14 The second woe passed and, behold, the third woe came quickly.

15 The seventh angel sounded his trumpet, a second time, and great voices in Heaven, said, The kingdoms of this world have become the kingdoms of our Lord and of his Christ, and he shall reign forever and ever.

16 The twenty-four elders who sat before God fell upon their faces and worshiped him.

18 The world's people were angry, but God's wrath had come, so the dead were judged and Christ gave rewards to his servants: the prophets, the saints, and those who feared his name.

Revelation 12

1-2 There appeared a great wonder in Heaven, a woman clothed with the sun. She was with child and cried from pain to be delivered.

3-4 There appeared another wonder in Heaven, a great red dragon. The dragon stood before the woman to devour her child as soon as it was born.

5 She brought forth a man-child, who was to rule all nations with a rod of iron, and her child was caught up to God and to his throne.

6 The woman fled into the wilderness where she had a place prepared by God. She was fed there 1260 days.

7-9 There was war in Heaven. Michael and his angels fought against the dragon, but he did not prevail. The great dragon, called the Devil and Satan, was cast down to earth along with his angels.

11 The believers overcame Satan by the blood of the Lamb and by the word of their testimony.

12-14 The devil came down, having great wrath because he knew that he had but a short time. So the dragon persecuted the woman, but the woman was given two wings to fly into the wilderness for three and a half years.

17 The dragon was furious with the woman and went to make war with the remnant of her seed who kept the commandments of God and had the testimony of Jesus Christ.

Revelation 13

1 I saw a beast rise up out of the sea, having seven heads and ten horns with ten crowns. And upon his seven heads was the name of blasphemy.

2 The dragon gave the beast his power, his seat, and great authority.

3 One of his heads looked like it was wounded to death, but was healed. All the world followed after this beast.

4 The people worshiped the dragon who gave power to the beast.

5 He had a mouth speaking great things and blasphemies, and power was given to him to continue forty-two months.

6 He opened his mouth in blasphemy against God and those in Heaven.

7 He planned to make war with the saints and to overcome them.

8 His plan was that all who dwell upon the earth shall worship him, those whose names are not written in the Lamb's book of life.

9 If any man have an ear, let him hear.

11-12 I saw another beast coming up out of the earth. He had two horns like a lamb, and he spoke as a dragon. He exercised all the power of the first beast to cause all people to worship the first beast.

13-15 He did great wonders, so that he made fire come down to the earth from Heaven in the sight of men. He deceived by means of his miracles, and he demanded that all people make a graven image of the beast. He had power to give life to the image, so it spoke out and killed those who would not worship it.

16-17 He caused all people to receive a mark in their right hand or forehead. No man could buy or sell, except those who had the mark, name, or the number of his name.

18 Here is wisdom; let him who has understanding count the number of the beast, for it is the number of a man, and his number is 666.

Revelation 14

1 I looked, and a Lamb stood on mount Zion. With him were 144,000 persons who had God's name written on their foreheads.

3 They sang a new song before the throne, the four beasts, and the elders. No man could learn their song except those who were the redeemed.

4 These were the ones who were not defiled with women, for they were virgins. They followed the Lamb wherever he went.

6 I saw another angel fly about in Heaven having the everlasting gospel to preach to those who dwell on the earth.

8 A second angel followed, saying twice, Babylon is fallen, is fallen, because she made all nations drink of the wine of the wrath of her fornication.

9 -11 A third angel followed them, saying with a loud voice, If any man worship the beast and his image and receive his mark in his forehead or in

his hand, the same shall drink of the wine of the wrath of God. He shall be tormented with fire and brimstone in the presence of the holy angels and the Lamb forever and ever, and they shall have no rest day or night.

12 In Heaven are those who keep the commandments of God and faith in Jesus.

14-15 I looked and saw a white cloud. Upon the cloud sat one like the Son of Man, having on his head a golden crown and in his hand a sharp sickle. Another angel came out of the temple crying with a loud voice, Thrust in your sickle and reap, for the time has come to reap the ripe harvest of earth.

16 He thrust in his sickle on the earth and the earth, was reaped.

Revelation 15

1 I saw another sign in Heaven, seven angels having the seven last plagues. In their vials was the wrath of God.

6 Seven angels, clothed in pure white linen and wearing golden girdles, came out of the temple with seven plagues.

8 The temple was filled with smoke from the glory and power of God. No man was able to enter into the temple until the seven plagues were fulfilled.

Revelation 16

1 I heard a great voice come out of the temple saying to the seven angels, Go and pour out the vials of the wrath of God upon the earth.

2 The first went and poured out his vial. Smelly and painful sores fell upon the men who had the mark of the beast and worshiped his image.

3 The second angel poured out his vial. The sea became like the blood of a dead man, and every living soul died in the sea.

4 The third angel poured out his vial. The rivers and fountains of waters became blood.

8-9 The fourth angel poured out his vial upon the sun. Power was given to him to scorch men with fire. But the scorched men blasphemed the name of God and repented not to give him glory.

10 The fifth angel poured out his vial upon the domain of the beast. The beast's kingdom was full of darkness, and its people chewed their tongues, due to the pain from the vial.

12 The sixth angel poured out his vial upon the great Euphrates River. It dried up to prepare the way for the kings of the east.

13 I saw an unclean spirit come out of the mouth of the dragon, the beast, and the false prophet.

14 The unclean spirits went out to the kings of the whole world to gather the people together to participate in the battle of that great day of God Almighty.

16 God gathered them together into a place called Armageddon.

17 The seventh angel poured out his vial into the air, and a great voice out of the temple of Heaven said, It is done.

18-20 There came a great earthquake. It divided the city, Babylon, into three parts, and the cities of the nations fell. God gave to Babylon the cup of the fierceness of his wrath. Every island and mountain disappeared.

21 Large hail, about the weight of a talent, fell upon men. They blasphemed God because of the plague.

Revelation 17

1 One of the seven angels who had the seven vials said, Come here; I will show you the judgment of the great whore who sits upon many waters.

3 So he carried me away in the spirit into the wilderness, and I saw a woman sit upon a scarlet colored beast, having seven heads and ten horns.

6 The woman was drunk with the blood of the saints and the martyrs of Jesus.

9, 12-14 This is for the mind who has wisdom. The seven heads are seven mountains on which the woman sits. The ten horns which I saw were ten kings, who had received no kingdom as yet, but for one hour they received power as if they had kingdoms with the beast. These have one mind and shall give their power and strength to the beast. These shall make war with the Lamb, and the Lamb shall overcome them, for he is Lord of lords, and King of kings. They who are with him are called, chosen and faithful.

17 God has put in their hearts these things to fulfil his will, to give their kingdoms to the beast until the words of God shall be fulfilled.

Revelation 18

1-2 After these things I saw another angel, having great power come down from Heaven. He cried with a strong voice, saying, Babylon the great is fallen, is fallen, and is become the habitation of devils and foul spirits.

4 I heard another voice from Heaven saying, Come out of her my people, so that you are not partakers of her sins and receive her plagues.

8 Her plagues came in one day. Death, mourning, and famine, for strong is the Lord God who judged her.

17 In one hour her great riches came to nothing.

21 A mighty angel took up a stone and cast it into the sea, saying, Thus with violence mercy shall that great city Babylon be thrown down and be no more.

Revelation 19   (The Millennium - 1000 years)

1-2 After Satan was defeated at the battle of Armageddon and God had avenged the wrongs committed against the Saints, I heard the voice of many

159

people in Heaven saying, Alleluia. Salvation, glory, honor, and power be
to the Lord our God. True and righteous are Christ's judgments, for he has
judged the great whore, Satan, who corrupted the earth with fornication. He
has avenged the blood of his servants.

5 An angel's voice came out from the heavenly throne, saying, Praise our
God, all you who are his servants and who fear him, both great and small.

6-7 I heard the voice of a great multitude, saying, Alleluia, for the Lord
God omnipotent (all powerful) reigns. Let us be glad and rejoice and give
honor to him, for the marriage of the Lamb (Christ) has come. His wife (the
believing saints, Christ's church) has made herself ready.

9 Blessed are they who are called to the marriage supper of the Lamb.

10 I fell at the angel's feet to worship him. And he said, You need not do
it; I am your fellow servant and of your brothers who have the testimony of
Jesus. Worship God, for the testimony of Jesus is the spirit of prophecy.

11 I saw Heaven open and saw a white horse. He that sat upon it was
called Faithful and True, and in righteousness he judged and made war.

13 His name was called The Word of God.

16 On his thigh was written, KING OF KINGS, AND LORD OF LORDS.

19 I saw the beast, the kings of the earth, and their armies, gathered together to make war against him and his army.

20 These were cast alive into a lake of fire burning with brimstone.

Revelation 20

1 I saw an angel come down from Heaven having the key to the bottomless pit and a great chain in his hand. He took hold of the dragon, that old
serpent, who is the Devil and Satan, and bound him a thousand years,

3 He cast Satan into the bottomless pit, shut him up, and set a seal upon
him, that he should not deceive the nations anymore until the thousand
years should be fulfilled, and after that he was released a little while.

4-5 I saw thrones and those who sat upon them, and judgment was given
to them. I saw those who were beheaded for the witness of Jesus and for the
Word of God, those who had not worshiped the beast nor received his mark.
They lived and reigned with Christ a thousand years. But the rest of the
dead lived not again until the thousand years was finished. This was the first
resurrection.

6 Blessed and holy are those who are in the first resurrection. They shall be
priests of God and Christ and shall reign with him a thousand years.

7-8 When the thousand years had passed, Satan was released from prison and
went out to deceive the nations of the earth, known as Gog and Magog, to do battle.

9 Gog and Magog surrounded the saints and the beloved city, but fire came
down from God out of Heaven and devoured them.

10 The devil that deceived them was cast into the lake of fire and brimstone

where the beast and the false prophet were, and they were tormented day and night forever and ever.

12 I saw the dead, small and great, stand before God, and the books were opened, and another book was opened which was the book of life. The dead were judged out of those things which were written in the books, according to their works.

14 Death and hell were cast into the lake of fire. This is the second death.

15 Whoever was not found written in the Lamb's book of life was cast into the lake of fire.

Revelation 21   (Eternity for the Saints)

1 I, John, saw a new Heaven and a new earth, for the first Heaven and the first earth were passed away, and there was no more sea.

2 I saw the holy city, the new Jerusalem, coming down from God out of Heaven prepared as a bride adorned for her husband.

3 I heard a great voice out of Heaven saying, Behold, the tabernacle of God is with men, and he will dwell with them, and they shall be his people, and God himself shall be with them and be their God.

4 God shall wipe away all tears from their eyes, and there shall be no more death, sorrow, crying, or pain, for the former things have passed away.

5 He that sat upon the throne said, Behold, I make all things new.

5-8 He said to me, These words are true and faithful. It is done. I am Alpha and Omega, the beginning and the end. He that overcomes shall inherit all things. I will be his God, and he shall be my son. The fearful, unbelieving, murderers, whore mongers, sorcerers, idolaters, and all liars, shall have their part in the lake which burns with fire and brimstone. This is the second death.

9 Then came to me one of the seven angels saying, Come here, and I will show you the bride, the Lamb's wife.

10 He carried me away in the spirit to a great high mountain and showed me that great city, the New Jerusalem, descending out of Heaven from God

16, 18-19, 21 The city was foursquare; the length, width, and height was twelve thousand furlongs. The walls were built of jasper, and the city was pure gold. The foundations of the wall of the city were garnished with all manner of precious stones. The twelve gates were twelve pearls.

22 I saw no temple in it, for the Lord God Almighty and the Lamb were the temple of it.

23, 25, 27 The city had no need of the sun or moon, for the glory of God and Christ lit it. The gates of it were not shut by day, for there was no night there. There was nothing in it that defiled it, only those whose names were written in the Lamb's book of life.

Revelation 22

1 The angel showed me a pure river of water of life proceeding out of the throne of God and of the Lamb.

2 In Heaven was the tree of life, which bore twelve fruits, whose leaves were for the healing of the nations.

3-4 There shall be no more curse, and his servants shall serve him and his name shall be in their foreheads.

7 Christ said, Behold, I come quickly; blessed is he that keeps the sayings of the prophecy of this book.

11 He that is unjust and filthy, let him be unjust and filthy still. He that is righteous and holy, let him be righteous and holy still.

13 I am the Alpha and Omega, the beginning and the end, the first and the last.

14 Blessed are those who do God's commandments, that they may have right to the tree of life.

16 I have sent my angel to testify to you these things. I am the root and the offspring of David and the bright and morning star.

17 The Spirit and the bride say, Come. And whosoever will, let him take the water of life freely.

18 If any man shall add to these things, God shall add to him the plagues that are written in this book.

21 The grace of our Lord Jesus Christ be with you all. Amen.

● ● ●

Memorize the Roman Road

Romans 3:23 All have sinned and fall short of the glory of God.

Romans 6:23 The wages of sin is death, but the gift of God is eternal life through Christ Jesus our Lord.

Romans 5:8 God demonstrated his love toward us, in that while we were yet sinners, Christ died for us.

Romans 10:9 If you confess with your mouth the Lord Jesus and believe in your heart that God has raised him from the dead, you will be saved.

Romans 10:10 For with the heart man believes to righteousness, and with the mouth confession is made to salvation.

Romans 10:13 For whosoever calls upon the name of the LORD shall be saved.

INDEX

Counselor - Isa 9: 6
covenant - Gen 17:7
corrupt - Ps 14:3
created - Gen 1:1
creation - Gen 2:2, Prov 8:22, Isa 44:25, Rom 8:22
Creator - Ecc 12:1
cross - Rom 8:17, 1 Cor 1:18
cross-dressing - Dt 22:5
crucified - Mk 16:6, Jn 20:25
damnation - Jn 5:29
damned - Mk 16:16
dancing - Ps 30:11, Ps 149:3
darkness - Is 9:2, Lk 12:3, Jn 3 19
David - Lk 1:33, Lk 20:44, Jn 7:42, Rom 1:3, Rev 21:16
Day of the Lord - Isa 29 :18, Joel 1:15, 1 Thes 5:2, 2 Pet 3:10
dead - Ps 115:17, Mt 8:22, Lk 9:60, Jn 11:25, Rom 6:4, Rom 6:8
death, dies - Ps 116:15, Prov 11:7, Jn 5:24, Jn 8:51, Rev 21:8
deceive - Mk 13:6
defense - Ps 94:22
deliver - 2 Sam 22:2, Ps 140:1
Devil - 1 Pet 5:8, Rev 12:12
divorced - Mt 5:32
divorcement - Mk 10:4
doctrine - 2 Jn 1:9
drinks - Isa 5: 22
drunk - Eph 5:18
earth - Jer 51:15
equal - 1 Sam 2:2
eternal God - Dt 33:27
eternal - Jn 17:3
eternal life - Jn 10:28
everlasting - Ps 90:2, Isa 9:6, Isa 40:28, Dan 12:2, Mt 25:46, Jn 6:47
evil - Ps 49:5, Ps 141:4, Prov 22: 8, Ecc 8:11, Isa 5:20, Rom 12:21, 1 Thes 5:22
exalt, exalted - Ps 57:5, Ps 99:5 , Ps 108:5
examine - 2 Cor 13:5
eyes - Ps 119:18
faith - Rom 1:17, Rom 3:28, Rom 5:1, Rom 10:17, Heb 11:1
false Christs - Mk 13: 22
false prophets - Mt 7: 15, Mt 24:11, Mt 24:24, Mk 13: \22
false teachers - Gal 4:17, 2 Pet 2:12
false witness - Prov 21: 28
father, fathers - Prov 23: 22, Mt 15:4, Eph 6:4, Col 3: 21
fear, fears - Ps 128:1, Prov 1:7, Ecc 8:12, Mt 10:28, Rev 14:7
first and the last - Isa 41:4, Isa 44:6, Isa 48:12, Rev 1: 17, Rev 21: 13
first fruits - Ex 23:19
flesh - Jn:3 6
follow me - Jn 12:26, Jn 21:19

fool, fools - Ps 53:1, Prov 10:21, Prov 12:20, Prov 23:9, Prov 29:11, Ecc 2:14
forever - Dan 4:34, Jn 6:58
forgive, forgiveness - Ps 86:5, Ps 130:4, Mt 18: 21, Jn 20:23
fornication - Mt 15:19, 1 Thes 4:3
fruit - Mt 3:10
fruit of the Spirit - Gal 5:22
genealogies - Titus 3:9
gifts - Rom 12:6 , 1 Cor 12:4
glory - Ps 19:1, Ps 104:31, Isa 42:8, Mt 25:31
God - Job 22:21, Ps 18:30, Ps 47:7, Isa 40:28, Isa 43:10, Isa 44:6, Isa 45:15,
    Ez 28:2, Jn 1:18, Jn 4:24, Jn 20:28, Acts 2:32
god, gods - Dt 6:14, 1 Chron 16:25, Ps 16:4, Ps 135:5, Josh 24:20
God is not a man - Num 23:19, Job 9:32, Ez 28:6, 9, Jn 4:24
godhead - Col 2:9
good - Ps 37:23, Ps 53:3, Ps 118:1, Isa 5:20, Micah 6:8, Mt 19:17, Mk 10:18
gospel - Rom 1:16, Rom 10:15
grace - 2 Cor 12:9, 2 Pet 3:18
grave - 1 Sam 2:6, Jn 5:29, 1 Ch 16:25
heal - Jer 17:14
heart - Ps 51:10
heaven - 1 Kings 8:27, Jn 21:18, 1 Pet 3:22
heir - Heb 1:2
hell - Mt 5:22, Mt 18:9, Mk 9:43
help - Ps 121:2, Ps 124:8
High Tower - 2 Sam 22:3
historical - Prov 22:28
holy - 1 Sam 2:2, Isa 5:16
Holy Ghost, Holy Spirit - Ps 51:10, Mt 3:11, Mt 12:31, Lk 3:16, Lk 12:12,
    Acts 2:4, Rom 15:13
homosexuality - Rom 1:26
hope - 1 Cor 13:13
house - Ps 122:1, Ps 127:1
husband, husbands - Eph 5:23, Col 3:19, 1 Pet 3:7
I am - Ex 3:14, Isa 43:13, Jn 8:24, Jn 8:58, Rev 1:8, Rev 21:13
Emmanuel - Isa 7:14, Mt 1:23, Jn 1:4, Jn 21:25
imputed - Rom 4:22
infinite - Ps 147:5
iniquities - Ps 90:8
interest - Prov 28:8
Israel - 1 Ch 16:36, Ps 73:1, Isa 41:14, Isa 45:17, Isa 52:12, Acts 2:36
Israelites - Jer 32:38
jealous - Ex 34:14, Dt 6:14, Josh 24:19, Nah 1:2
Jerusalem - Ps 129:5, Ps 132:13, Isa 33:20
Jews - Eph 2:18
judge, judges - 1 Sam 2:10, Ps 7:11, Ps 96:13, Mt 7:1, Acts 17:31
judgment day - Ps 37:13
judgment, judgments - Ps 19:9, Prov 28:5, Mt 5:21, Jn 5:27

poor - Prov 19:17, Prov 21: 17, Prov 22: 22, Mt 26:11
praise - Ps 7:17
pray - Mt 6:6, Lk 6:27, Eph 6:18, 1 Thes 5:17
prayer - Ps 143:1, Prov 28:9, Lk 19:46
pride - Prov 11:2, Prov 16:18
priesthood - Heb 7:24, 1 Pet 2:5, 1 Pet 2:9
prophets - Jer 14:14, Jer 23:25, Jer 23:30, Jer 27:9
propitiation - Rom 3:25, 1 Jn 4:10
prove - 2 Cor 13:5,
reconciled - 2 Cor 5:20
Redeemer - Job 19:25, Ps 19:14, Isa 41:14, Isa 44:24, Isa 48:17
refuge - Ps 46:1
repent, repentance - Mt 3:2, Acts 2:38, Rom 2:4, Rev 3:19
rich - Ps 49:16
righteous - Ps 37:16, Ps 92:12, Ps 129:4
righteousness - 2 Sam 22:25, Ps 85:10, Rom 4:3, Gal 5:5, Phil 3:9
rock - 2 Sam 22:2, Ps 62:2
rod - Prov 22: 15
safety - Prov 21: 31
saints - Rom 1:7, 1 Thes 3:13
salvation - Isa 12:2, Jonah 2:9, Acts 4:12, 1 Pet 1:9
sanctification - 1 Thes 4:3
sanctified - Acts 20:32
sanctify - 1 Pet 3:15
Satan - Lk 4:8, 2 Cor 11:14 .
saved - Mk 13:13, Jn 10:9, Rom 5:9, Rom 10:13
Savior - 2 Sam 22:3, Isa 43:3, Isa 45:15, Lk 2:11, Titus 1:4, Titus 3:6
savior - Isa 43:11, Hos 13:4
scripture - 2 Tim 3:16
second coming - 1 Thes 4:16
seek - Isa 48:6
separate - 2 Cor 6:17
serve - Ps 100:2
sex - Heb 13:4
sexually immorals - Rev 21:8
sheep - Isa 53:6
shepherd - Ps 23:1
sin, sins - Ps 4:4, Ps 130:3, Ecc 7:20, Isa 1:18, Isa 64:5, Zeph 3:5, Mk 2:7, Jn 16:9,
   Rom 5: 12, Rom 6:12, Rom 6:23, 2 Tim 1:19
sinners - Mt 9:13
sing - Ps 33:3, Ps 59:16, Ps 101:1
Son - Mt 11:27, Lk 10:22
son, sons - Prov 19:26, Jn 1:12
Son of God - 2 Cor 1:19
Son of Man - Mt 12:32, Lk 12:10
soul, souls - Gen 2:7, Ps 42:2, Ps 84:2, Ps 103:1, Prov 11:30, Prov 21:10, Mk 8:36,
   1 Cor 15:45
Spirit - Jn 3:6, Jn 4:24, Jn 6:63, Rom 8:26, 2 Cor 3:17, 1 Thes 5:19, 1 Pet 1:22, Rev 22:17